50 Pincushions to Knit and Crochet

50 Pincushions to Knit and Crochet

CAT THOMAS

Search Press

A QUARTO BOOK

Published in 2014 by Search Press Ltd
Wellwood
North Farm Road
Tunbridge Wells
Kent TN2 3DR

ISBN 978-1-78221-023-8

Conceived, designed and produced by
Quarto Publishing plc
The Old Brewery
6 Blundell Street
London N7 9BH

Project Editor: Chelsea Edwards
Designer: Julie Francis
Photographers: Laura Forrester and
  Nicki Dowey (pages 52 and 53)
Photography Assistant: Rose Martin
Pattern Checker: Rachel Vowles
Illustrator: Kuo Kang Chen
Proofreader: Chloe Todd Fordham
Indexer: Helen Snaith
Art Director: Caroline Guest

Creative Director: Moira Clinch
Publisher: Paul Carslake

Colour separation in Singapore by
  Pica Digital Pte Limited

Printed in China by 1010 Printing
  International Limited

Contents

Foreword

One of my first roles in life was to pick up pins for my mother who was an avid knitter and crocheter. My earliest childhood memories involve making pincushions.

From this childhood beginning I've learned that skills are best developed through fun pieces rather than by tester squares. There's no more rewarding way to master a new technique than to have a finished item at the end of it.

About This Book

Pick a Pincushion **35**

An Arrangement
• see page 68 for crochet pattern

Opposite: Clockwise from top left

Polka Dots
• see page 60 for knitting pattern

Tangerine Dream
• see page 122 for crochet pattern

Round and Around
• see page 88 for crochet pattern

Flower Power
• see page 80 for crochet pattern

See the finished pieces in 'Pick a Pincushion' (pages 22–55) to help you decide which patterns you want to work on.

Each pincushion is labelled with its name, page reference and whether it is knitted or crocheted.

This book gives you just that opportunity; it's bursting with fun and pretty pincushions for you to get stuck in to. Mixing the traditional, the quirky and the seasonal, it creates a bit of a pincushion dilemma. Which one to start first?

Cat Thomas

This key denotes the skill level required for each pattern.
One yarn ball = Beginner
Two yarn balls = Intermediate
Three yarn balls = Advanced

Photographs of the finished pincushion show you what you should be aiming for.

Here in 'Pincushion Patterns' (pages 56–125) you'll find all the instructions you'll need to complete the pictured pincushion.

---

78 Circus Time • Crochet

Circus Time

Add circus flair to your craft table. Combining triangles and octagons, this pincushion also has an appliqué star for a fairground feel.

SKILL LEVEL

Tools & Materials
DK mercerised cotton:
Blue: 25.5m (28yds)
Green: 15.25m (18½yds)
Red: 10.75m (11½yds)
Cream: 2.5m (100in)
Crochet hook: 2.75mm (US size C)
2 foam pieces, 2.5cm (1in) thick, to match the finished shape

Green triangles
Make six 10-chain triangles.
Row 1: Ch11, dc in second st from hook, dc in all sts, ch1, turn. (10 dc)
Row 2: Dc2tog, dc in next 6 sts, dc2tog, ch1, turn.
Row 3: Dc in all sts, ch1, turn. (8 dc)
Row 4: Dc2tog, dc in next 4 sts, dc2tog, ch1, turn.
Row 5: Dc in all sts, ch1, turn. (6 dc)
Row 6: Dc2tog, dc in next 2 sts, dc2tog, ch1, turn.
Row 7: Dc in all sts, ch1, turn. (4 dc)
Row 8: Dc2tog twice, ch1, turn.
Row 9: Dc in both sts, ch1, turn. (2 dc)
Row 10: Dc2tog.
Fasten off leaving a tail for sewing in.

Red triangles
Make six 8-chain triangles.
Row 1: Ch9, dc in second st from hook, dc in all sts, ch1, turn. (8 dc)
Row 2: Dc2tog, dc in next 4 sts, dc2tog, ch1, turn.
Row 3: Dc in all sts, ch1, turn. (6 dc)
Row 4 Dc2tog, dc in next 2 sts, dc2tog, ch1, turn.
Row 5: Dc in all sts, ch1, turn. (4 dc)
Row 6: Dc2tog twice, ch1, turn.
Row 7: Dc in both sts, ch1, turn. (2 dc)
Row 8: Dc2tog.
Fasten off leaving a tail for sewing in.

Hexagon base
Begin with a sliding loop.
Round 1: Slip st, ch3 (counts as first tr), 11dc in ring, slip st to top of ch3, pull loop shut. (12 tr)
Round 2: Ch3, 3tr in next st, (tr in next st, 3tr in next st) 5 times, slip st to top of ch3. (24 tr)
Round 3: Ch3, tr in next st, 3tr in next st, (tr in next 3 sts, 3tr in next st) 5 times, tr in next st, slip st to top of ch3. (36 tr)
Round 4: Ch3, tr in next 2 sts, 3tr in next st, (tr in next 5 sts, 3tr in next st) 5 times, tr in next 3 sts, slip st to top of ch3. (48 tr)
Round 5: Ch3, tr in next 3 sts, 3tr in next st, (tr in next 7 sts, 3tr in next st) 5 times, tr in next 3 sts, slip st to top of ch3. (60 tr)

Hexagon top
Begin with a sliding loop.
Round 1: Slip st, ch3 (counts as first tr), 11dc in ring, slip st to top of ch3, pull loop shut. (12 tr)
Round 2: Ch3, 3tr in next st, (tr in next st, 3tr in next st) 5 times, slip st to top of ch3. (24 tr)
Round 3: Ch3, 1tr in next st, 3tr in next st, (tr in next 3 sts, 3tr in next st) 5 times, tr in next st, slip st to top of ch3. (36 tr)
Round 4: (Worked in exactly the same way as base Round 4 but substituting tr for htr): ch2 (counts as first htr), htr in next 2 sts, 3htr in next st, (htr in next 5 sts, 3htr in next st) 5 times, htr in next 2 sts, slip st to top of ch3. (48 htr)

Crochet • Circus Time 79

Star
Begin with a sliding loop.
Round 1: Slip st, dc, (tr, picot3, tr, dc) 4 times, tr, picot3, tr, in the ring, slip st to first ch, pull loop shut.
Fasten off leaving a long tail for sewing to the top.

Assembly and finishing
Sew the star to the top.
With the top facing, attach to the base of the red triangles using a double crochet join. The corners of the triangles should meet the corners of the hexagon top.
Sew a cream cross stitch star on each green triangle.

Attach the first two rows of the green triangles together starting at the base before joining to the red triangle with a backstitch on the reverse. This forms the sides of the shape.
Weave in all loose ends.
Cut the foam to match the size of the shape. Depending on the depth of the sides you might need two pieces. These can be tapered so that they are narrower at the top.
Insert the foam. Pin the base to the side section matching the corners of the hexagon to the triangle joins. Attach the base to the green triangles using a double crochet join.

Double crochet join the red triangles to the base hexagon

Join the red and green triangles together to create the side section

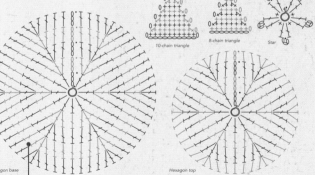

10-chain triangle   8-chain triangle   Star

Hexagon base

Hexagon top

This list provides all the information you need for selecting your equipment and materials.

Knit (where relevant) and crochet charts are included in addition to the written instructions.

Eyelash yarn

DK chenille

Chunky cotton

4-ply merino and cashmere mixture

4-ply wool and nylon mixture

DK wool and cotton mixture

DK cotton

Pearl cotton

Mohair

Materials and Equipment

The neat thing about making pincushions is that they don't require specialist tools, nor do they use much yarn.

Yarns

Yarns are available in a range of weights, from very fine to extra chunky. Because yarns may vary from one manufacturer to another and certainly change from one fibre to another, only generic yarn types are indicated for the pincushions in this book. You should be aware of the properties of different yarns, however, from the fullness of cotton to the elasticity of wool, because the construction of a yarn will affect its behaviour and characteristics, and so will influence the end result. Try using different tensions and, if in doubt, use a smaller needle/hook size than usual.

Separate your yarns into colour groups and keep these in transparent plastic containers so that you have a palette of colours to work with.

Knitting needles are available in a variety of sizes and materials.

Knitting needles

Needle sizes are specified for each pincushion. Pairs of knitting needles are made in a variety of lengths. Most are aluminium, although larger-size needles are made of plastic to reduce their weight. For most of the designs in this book, a conventional pair of needles is used, but double-pointed needles are used in some of the projects.

Crochet hooks

Crochet hooks are available in a wide range of sizes and materials. Most hooks are made from aluminium or plastic. Small sizes of steel hooks are made for working with very fine yarns. Handmade wooden, bamboo and horn hooks are also available.

Hook sizes are quoted differently in Europe and the United States, and some brands of hook are labelled with more than one numbering system. Choosing a hook is largely a matter of personal preference. The design of the hook affects the ease of working considerably. Look for a hook that has a comfortable grip.

Stuffing materials and additional equipment

There are a number of options open to you when it comes to stuffing your pincushion. The most suitable choice has been suggested for each individual pincushion.

Polyester hollowfibre filling is a synthetic stuffing that is extremely lightweight and also washable. It has a soft feel and it bounces back into shape. It tends to clump less than many of the other stuffing materials. It is also widely available.

Cotton wadding is available in roll form. It can be cut into shape and it is ideal for pincushions where a light padding is desired. Wadding adheres to itself, allowing it to be stacked or layered. Loose hollowfibre filling can be inserted between the layers for added shape that won't move.

Foam is a high-density filling that allows you to make more structured pincushions. There are many different weights of foam. Upholstery foam is

Assorted crochet hooks

available in 2.5cm (1in) sheets and can be easily cut to fit whatever shape is required by your design.

The weight of your pincushion is a personal choice. If you prefer a heavier weight you might consider crushed walnut shells, coarse sand, split peas or lentils as your filling material.

Adding dried lavender or rose petals to the filling will release subtle perfume as the pins are stuck into the cushion.

TAPE MEASURE

Essential for measuring lengths of yarn, choose one that features both centimetres and inches on the same side.

MARKERS AND ROW COUNTERS

Readymade markers can be used to indicate a repeat or to help count stitches in a chain. Similarly, a row counter may help you to keep track of the number of rows you have worked, but in knitting this is usually easy if you remember to include the stitches on the needle as a row.

A tape measure lets you check that you have adequate yarn.

Row counters are useful.

Always have a sharp pair of scissors handy.

Crochet Symbols

Key to symbols used in charts

Basic symbols

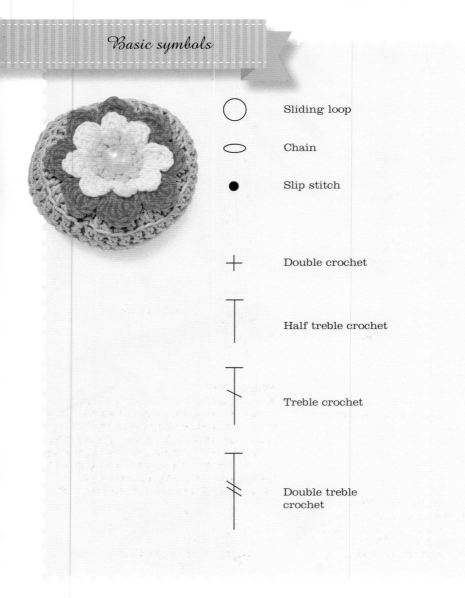

◯   Sliding loop

⬭   Chain

●   Slip stitch

+   Double crochet

⊤   Half treble crochet

Treble crochet

Double treble crochet

Work in the single front strand of the stitch below – this concave curve will appear underneath the stitch symbol, for example: slip stitch in front strand of stitch below.

Work in the single back strand of the stitch below – this convex curve will appear underneath the stitch symbol, for example: double crochet in back strand of stitch below.

►   An arrowhead indicates the beginning of a row or round where this is not immediately apparent.

Increases

Symbols joined at the base show stitches worked in a single stitch or space to make an increase. They are usually described as 'work so many stitches in the next stitch', or at the beginning of a row, 'work so many stitches in the stitch below'.

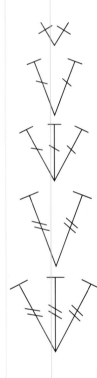

2-st dc increase

2-st tr increase

3-st tr increase

2-st dtr increase

3-st dtr increase

Decreases

Symbols joined at the top show stitches gathered into one stitch to form a decrease. Each stitch of the group (tr, dtr, etc, according to the symbol) is made without working the last wrap (a wrap is yarn round hook, then pull yarn through loop). This leaves one loop on the hook for each incomplete stitch plus the original loop. The decrease is completed by taking the yarn round the hook and then pulling the yarn through all loops on the hook.

2-st dc decrease

2-st tr decrease

3-st tr decrease

2-st dtr decrease

trtr and dtr decrease

Wraps

A wrap is yarn round hook, then pull yarn through loop (see above its use in decreasing). In colour changing, working the last wrap of a stitch with the new colour makes a neat change-over.

Clusters

A cluster is made exactly like a decrease (see left) except that the stitches are all worked in a single stitch or space before being gathered together at the top.

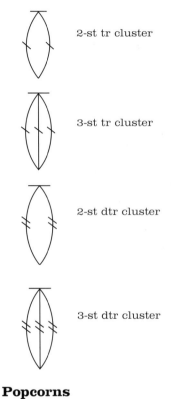

2-st tr cluster

3-st tr cluster

2-st dtr cluster

3-st dtr cluster

Popcorns

A popcorn is worked in one stitch like a cluster (see above), but the stitches are gathered together differently at the top. Work the stitches, then slip the last loop off the hook. Reinsert the hook in the top of first stitch of the group, as instructed, then catch the empty loop and pull it through to close the top of the popcorn.

5-st tr popcorn

Abbreviations

Knitting abbreviations

k	knit
kfb	knit in front and back of stitch to make two stitches from one
mb	make bobble as specifed in pattern
m1	make a stitch by lifting strand between stitches from front and knit in back of strand
m1f	make 1 front: as m1, noting that new stitch slants to the left
m1b	make 1 back: make a stitch by lifting strand between stitches from back and knit in front of it to make a stitch that slants to the right
m1p	make a stitch by lifting strand between stitches from front and purl in back of strand
p	purl
psso	pass slipped stitch over
RS	right side(s)
skpo	slip one stitch knitwise, knit one, pass slipped stitch over
sk2po	slip one knitwise, knit two together, pass slipped stitch over
sl	slip

st(s)	stitch(es)
st st	stocking stitch
tbl	through the back of the loop(s)
tog	together
WS	wrong side(s)
wyab	with yarn at back
wyif	with yarn in front
yo	yarn forward and over needle to make a stitch

Crochet abbreviations

ch	chain
ch sp	chain space
dc	double crochet
dec	decrease
dtr	double treble crochet
htr	half treble crochet
lp	loop(s)
RS	right side(s)
sp	space
ss	slip stitch
st(s)	stitch(es)
tog	together
tr	treble crochet
trtr	triple treble crochet
WS	wrong side(s)
yo	yarn over hook
yrh	yarn round hook

Crochet and knitting abbreviations

( )	round brackets indicate a group of stitches to be worked in one place or a specified number of times
* **	asterisks mark a section of instructions to be repeated

Notes on Knitting

This section is not a lesson in knitting; it is simply a reminder of a few basics, together with a few suggestions and techniques that might be new to an inexperienced knitter.

Slipknot

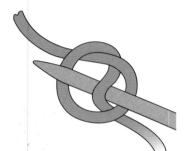

1 Putting a slipknot on the needle makes the first stitch of the cast-on. Loop the yarn around two fingers of the left hand, the ball end on top. Dip the needle into the loop, catch the ball end of the yarn and pull it through the loop.

2 Pull the ends of the yarn to tighten the knot. Tighten the ball end to bring the knot up to the needle.

Casting on

There are several cast-on methods, each with their own merits.

THUMB METHOD

Sometimes called long-tail cast-on, this uses a single needle and produces an elastic edge.

1 Leaving an end about three times the length of the required cast-on, put a slipknot on the needle. Holding the yarn end in the left hand, take the left thumb under the yarn and upwards. Insert the needle in the loop made on the thumb.

2 Use the ball end of the yarn to make a knit stitch, slipping the loop off the thumb. Pull the yarn end to close the stitch up to the needle. Continue making stitches in this way. The result looks like a row of garter stitch because the yarn has been knitted off the thumb.

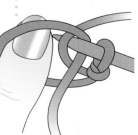

CABLE CAST-ON

This two-needle method gives a firm edge with the appearance of a rope.

1 Put a slipknot on one needle. Use the other needle and the ball end of the yarn to knit into the loop on the left-hand needle without slipping it off. Transfer the new stitch to the left-hand needle.

2 Insert the right-hand needle between the new stitch and the next stitch, and then make another stitch as before. Continue making stitches in this way.

KNITTED CAST-ON

Make a cable cast-on as above, but instead of knitting between stitches, insert the right-hand needle in the front of each stitch in the usual way. This gives a softer edge than the cable method.

i-cord

A very useful round cord can be made using two double-pointed needles.

Cast on three (or the required number of) stitches and knit one row in the usual way. * Without turning, slide the stitches to the opposite end of the needle. Take the yarn firmly across the wrong side from left to right and knit one row. Repeat from * for the required length.

Notes on Crochet

Understanding how to make simple stitches is the key to constructing interesting shapes in crochet. Here are a few reminders of some basics and some suggestions for building on them.

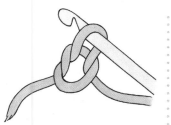

Slipknot

1 Putting a slipknot on the hook makes the first loop of the chain that will hold the stitches of the first row or round. Loop the yarn around two fingers of the left hand, the ball end to the front. Insert the hook in the loop, catch the ball end of the yarn and pull it through the loop.

2 Pull the ends of yarn to tighten the knot. Now tighten the ball end to bring the knot up to the hook.

Hooking action

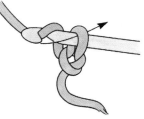

Hold the slipknot (and later the chain) between the thumb and forefinger of the left hand. Take the yarn over the second finger of the left hand so it is held taut. Take it around the little finger as well if necessary. The right hand is then free to manipulate the hook. With a turn of the wrist, guide the tip of the hook under the yarn. Catch the yarn and pull it through the loop on the hook to make a chain.

Hooking and catching is referred to as yarn round hook (abbreviation: yrh). It is the action used in making a chain, a slip stitch and, in various combinations, all other crochet stitches.

Note Unless the instructions state otherwise, the hook should be inserted under the two strands of yarn that form the top of the chain, or the top of the stitch.

Rounds

Rounds are started in a chain ring, or in a sliding loop for a tighter centre, and are worked in an anticlockwise direction without turning over.

CHAIN RING

Join a number of chain stitches into a ring with a slip stitch in the first chain. Work the first round of stitches around the chain and into the centre. If the yarn end is also worked around, the ring is lightly padded and this end can be pulled to tighten it.

SLIDING LOOP

1 To make a sliding loop, first coil the yarn around two fingers and then use the hook to pull through a loop of the ball end of the yarn, as if making a slipknot (see left, step 1). However, do not then pull the yarn tight. Holding the loop flat between the thumb and forefinger of the left hand, catch the yarn and pull it through the loop on the hook to anchor it.

2 Working under two strands of yarn each time, make the stitches as directed and then pull the free yarn end to close the sliding loop. Join the ring of stitches with a slip stitch in the first stitch.

Joining and Stuffing

Pincushions are usually constructed from two or more pieces sandwiched around a filling. Using the joining and stuffing methods here will make your work look carefully crafted. Creating a professional-looking pincushion with a clean edge is all about the finishing. Using the same yarn and hook or needle size will provide continuity.

Crochet joins

Pieces can be attached either with a crochet join or by sewing. In both methods the join is worked through the inner loops when the pieces are pinned with wrong sides together.

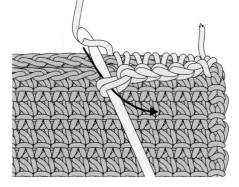

DOUBLE CROCHET JOIN

With wrong sides together, insert the hook through the back loop on the front piece and then into the nearest loop on the back piece. Draw the yarn through so that there are two loops on the hook. Slide the yarn over the hook and draw through the two loops.

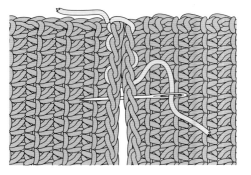

JOINING HORIZONTAL ROWS

Using either the slipstitch or double crochet method, work into the sides of the stitches on each side, evenly spacing the stitches close together to avoid gaps.

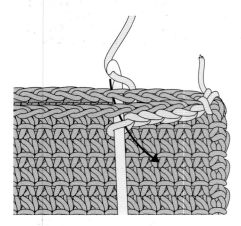

CROCHET SLIPSTITCH

Place the pieces with the wrong sides together. Insert the hook through the back loop on the front piece and then into the nearest loop on the back piece. These are the two inner loops. Draw the yarn through the stitch on the hook. Work in each stitch in turn.

For corners, three stitches can be worked into one stitch for a pronounced turn.

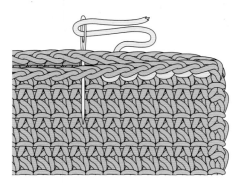

SEWN SLIPSTITCH

This is used when joining motifs together and is worked in a zigzag manner.

With a blunt-ended needle, insert it through the centre of a stitch and then through the stitch on the opposite piece, and draw the yarn through the back of the next stitch on the first piece.

Knit joins

Here are a few methods for joining the side seams.

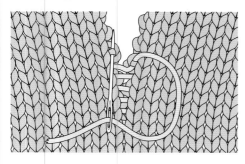

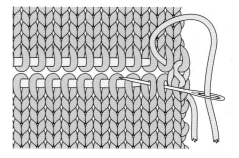

MATTRESS STITCH ON STOCKINETTE STITCH

Place the pieces with right sides facing. Using a blunt-ended needle, insert it under the horizontal bar between the first two stitches on one side. Then insert it under the bar between the same stitches on the opposite side. Draw the yarn through. Repeat for each stitch.

MATTRESS STITCH ON GARTER STITCH

Place the pieces with right sides facing. Using a blunt-ended needle, insert it through the bottom of the 'bump' on the end of the row and then the top of the 'bump' on the opposite side. Draw the yarn through.

GRAFTING

This method is used to join the cast-on and cast-off edges.

Working with right sides together so that the edges butt up together, insert the needle and come out of the centre of the first stitch just above the edge. Insert through the middle of the stitch on the other side. Pull the yarn through. This will appear to be working through the back of the V stitch on each side.

Stuffing your pincushion

If you are using a loose stuffing such as hollowfibre filling, it is best to stuff as you go. This is easier than trying to poke the stuffing through a small opening at the end.

Take small amounts of stuffing and pull the fibres apart before placing in the pincushion or fabric casing. As more stuffing is placed inside, ensure that it reaches the edges and corners. You can prevent lumps by continuously filling rather than having breaks in the fibre.

If the stuffing becomes lumpy or starts clumping together, pull it out and start over.

To ensure an even distribution, use the blunt end of a knitting needle or chopstick to move the stuffing around until you are happy.

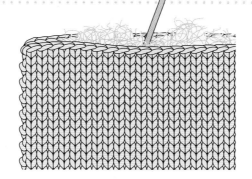

Fabric inserts

Lacy or open-weave pincushions will need to have the filling inserted in a casing so that it doesn't poke through the openwork. Experiment with matching or contrasting materials with a closed weave for an individual look. Try silk, cotton or linen.

MAKING A COTTON INSERT

A simple casing can be made using a fabric with a medium weave to keep the filling in.

Using one side of the finished pincushion as a template, draw around it on fabric using a water- or air-erasable pen. Cut out two pieces of the fabric, and add extra for a seam allowance.

If using a sewing machine, stitch around the shape leaving a gap on one side. If sewing by hand, use a backstitch to make the seam. Turn the fabric inside out and stuff. Sew the gap with slipstitch.

FELT INSERT

If the motif is open and the rest of the pincushion has a firmer weave, a felt insert can be used to contain the filling.

Draw around the motif on toning felt. Cut around the felt shape. The insert can be slipstitched to the reverse of the motif.

Embroidery Guide

On occasion, the knit and crochet pincushions in this book have been further embellished with various decorative stitches. To help you re-create these sweet motifs and effects, here are the most commonly used hand stitches.

Before beginning your embroidery you need to secure the thread. This can be done with a double stitch on the reverse of the knit or crochet piece. The tail of the thread can be woven in the back of the row.

When stitching on knitted or crocheted fabric, make sure the needle is worked into the gaps between stitches so the yarn does not split.

Running stitch

This is the most basic embroidery stitch. It is very simple to do and can look very effective on a knitted fabric if used in the right way with good yarns.

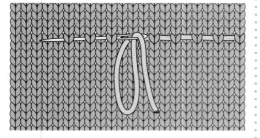

Bring the needle through from the back of the work, then insert it through the piece from front to back a short distance to the left. Bring the needle through from back to front again, a short distance to the left, ensuring that the stitches are of similar size.

Backstitch

This stitch is a good stitch for joining seams and it is also useful for creating outlining and lines.

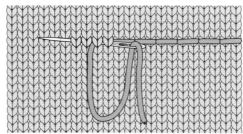

Bring the needle through from the back of the work. From the front and in one motion, take the needle through to the back a short distance along to the right, then draw back through the work to the front the same distance along to the left from the beginning of the stitch

Continue from right to left by inserting the needle through from front to back at the point where the last stitch emerged.

Stem stitch

This creates a line of stitching that can travel in any direction; it is useful for outlining motifs and is worked like backstitch, except that the yarns overlap.

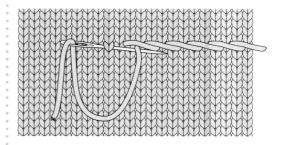

Bring the needle through from the back of the work, then insert it through the piece from front to back, a short distance to the right at a slight angle. The distance will depend on how large you wish the stitch to be.

Cross-stitch

Traditionally, cross-stitch is worked on a canvas following a pattern drawn out on a grid. The cross-stitch occupies the space of one or a multiple of squares on the grid.

Cross-stitch works particularly well on a knitted fabric because the knitted stitches are a constant shape and size, making it easy to track and complete complicated patterns.

Chain stitch

As with stem stitch, running stitch and blanket stitch, chain stitch creates a line and can be worked horizontally, vertically or in the shape of a curve. Chain stitch is worked in much the same way as blanket stitch in that the loop of the yarn is wrapped around the sewing needle before the stitch is completed.

Buttonhole stitch

This stitch can reinforce the edge of a knitted fabric and reduces the likelihood of the fabric edge curling. It is also a good stitch to use to apply appliqué or additional knitted pieces.

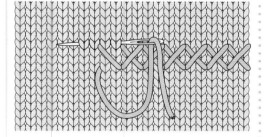
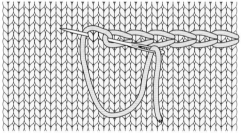
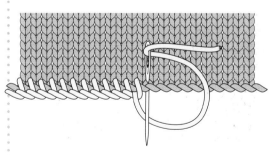

Work across one or two stitches and rows as required. Bring the yarn through from the back and make a diagonal stitch to the upper left corner of the 'grid'. Bring the needle back through to the front at the top right corner, and take the yarn back through the work from back to front and make a diagonal stitch to the bottom left corner.

Bring the needle through from the back. * In one motion, take the yarn through from front to back at the point where the first yarn came through to the front, to create a loop. Bring the needle back through to the front a short distance along to the left and through the centre of the loop. Tighten and repeat from *.

Working from left to right, bring the needle through the piece from the back, approximately one row in from the edge of the fabric. From the front, thread the needle through to the back, one stitch to the right, point the needle upwards, catch the loop of the yarn around it and pull through.

Lazy daisy

A quick way of creating the appearance
of a knitted flower is to sew a lazy daisy.
This stitch is a variation on chain stitch.

Satin stitch

Satin stitch is a very firm embroidery
method and is used to cover the knitted
stitches completely. It is a good stitch to
use to fill spaces outlined by a stem
stitch, for example. Be careful not to pull
the stitches too tightly, since this will
cause puckering.

French knot

French knots can add a three-
dimensional aspect to embroidery on a
knitted fabric. They look especially good
as flower centres.

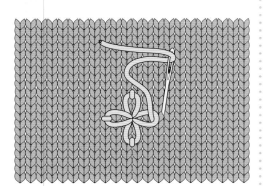

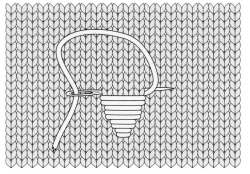

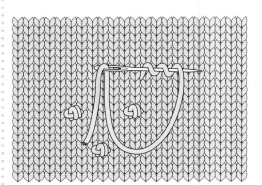

Make a chain stitch as described on page
19, but instead of making a running
sequence of stitches, sew a small stitch
over the top of the chain to hold the loop
in place. Repeat this in the formation of
a small flower, each chain representing
one petal.

Make small stitches at a slight angle as
close together as possible, by bringing
the yarn through from the back and
then from front to back the required
distance away.

Bring the needle through the work from
back to front. Wrap the yarn around the
needle once or twice, then take the needle
through to the back as close to where the
yarn first came through as possible.

Bullion knots

This is a variation on a French knot and is worked in much the same way.

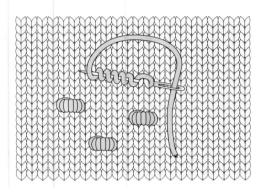

Bring the needle through the work from back to front. Thread the needle through from front to back at the point where the yarn emerged, then back to the front, one stitch (or the required length) to the left. Do not bring the needle all the way through. Wrap the yarn around the sewing needle five or six times. Hold the yarn firmly and pull the needle through. Pull to tighten. Thread the needle through to the back at the point where the very first stitch emerged.

CHAPTER 1

Pick a Pincushion

Browse through this beautiful directory to help you select your next pincushion project. Whether the pincushion is for yourself or you're making it as a gift, it's easy to choose one that's perfect for you.

Buttoned Down Granny
» see page 92 for crochet pattern

Sweet Lavender

» see page 83 for knitting pattern

Got It Covered
» see page 112 for crochet pattern

Opposite: Clockwise from top left

From Little Acorns
» see page 82 for knitting pattern

Scaredy Cat
» see page 84 for crochet pattern

Diagonal Square
» see page 121 for knitting pattern

Coffee and Cream
» see page 101 for crochet pattern

Beehive
» see page 102 for crochet pattern

Flora
» see page 116 for crochet pattern

Opposite: Clockwise from top left

Taste of Honey
» see page 113 for knitting pattern

Button Stripes
» see page 73 for knitting pattern

Fly Away Home
» see page 117 for crochet pattern

Dala Horse
» see page 66 for knitting pattern

Daisy, Daisy
» see page 94 for crochet pattern

Pear
» see page 77 for knitting pattern

An Arrangement
» see page 68 for crochet pattern

Opposite: Clockwise from top left

Polka Dots
» see page 60 for knitting pattern

Tangerine Dream
» see page 122 for crochet pattern

Round and Around
» see page 88 for crochet pattern

Flower Power
» see page 80 for crochet pattern

Chequered Heart
» see page 120 for knitting pattern

Ice Blue
» see page 100 for crochet pattern

Opposite: Clockwise from top left

Water Lily
» see page 114 for crochet pattern

Pocketful of Lace
» see page 67 for knitting pattern

Cupcake
» see page 62 for crochet pattern

Ammonite
» see page 65 for crochet pattern

Flower Mandala
» see page 108 for crochet pattern

Opposite: Clockwise from top left

Ribbon Lace
» see page 118 for crochet pattern

Mint Stripe
» see page 123 for crochet pattern

Fuchsia
» see page 74 for crochet pattern

Seed Pearls
» see page 61 for knitting pattern

Dianthus Pinks
» see page 87 for crochet pattern

Azulejo
» see page 109 for crochet pattern

Chain of Flowers
» see page 98 for crochet pattern

Got to Love Cats
» see page 104 for knitting pattern

Stellar
» see page 81 for knitting pattern

Opposite: Clockwise from top left

Reindeer
» see page 96 for knitting pattern

Cornflower
» see page 86 for crochet pattern

Mr Bear
» see page 106 for crochet pattern

Deep Water
» see page 99 for knitting pattern

Flower Meadow

» see page 71 for knitting pattern

Parterre Garden
» see page 70 for crochet pattern

From the Vine
» see page 64 for crochet pattern

Opposite: Clockwise from top left

Snow in Summer
» see page 97 for knitting pattern

Unstuck
» see page 90 for crochet pattern

Bubbles
» see page 93 for crcchet pattern

Under the Stars: Gemini
» see page 124 for crochet pattern

CHAPTER 2

Pincushion Patterns

This chapter contains all the instructions from the first stitch through to the finishing touches that you'll need for creating your perfect pincushion. Each pattern has a skill level rating and a list of equipment and materials you will require.

A Forest

'A Forest' is a geometric, abstract pincushion that takes inspiration from mid-20th century design. Put a contemporary twist on the tonal colours to make it fresh and modern.

SKILL LEVEL

Tools & Materials

DK mercerised cotton:
Lime green: 36.6m (40yds), make 3
Emerald green: 5.6m (6yds), make 2
Blue: 5.6m (6yds), make 2
Grey: 2.8m (3yds), make 1
Aqua: 2.8m (3yds), make 1

Crochet hook: 2.25mm
(US size 1/0)
Hollowfibre filling

Front

Make nine small triangles.

Row 1: Ch11, dc in second st from hook, dc in all sts, ch1, turn. (10 dc)

Row 2: Dc2tog, dc in next 6 sts, dc2tog, ch1, turn.

Row 3: Dc in all sts, ch1, turn. (8 dc)

Row 4: Dc2tog, dc in next 4 sts, dc2tog, ch1, turn.

Row 5: Dc in all sts, ch1, turn. (6 dc)

Row 6: Dc2tog, dc in next 2 sts, dc2tog, ch1, turn.

Row 7: Dc in all sts, ch1, turn. (4 dc)

Row 8: Dc2tog twice, ch1, turn.

Row 9: Dc in both sts, ch1, turn. (2 dc)

Row 10: Dc2tog.

Fasten off leaving a tail for sewing.

Back

Make one, using lime green.

Row 1: Ch 32, ch1, dc in second st from hook, dc in all sts, ch1, turn. (32 dc)

Row 2: Dc2tog, dc in next 28 sts, dc2tog, ch1, turn.

Row 3: Dc in all sts, ch1, turn. (30 dc)

Row 4: Dc2tog, dc in next 26 sts, dc2tog, ch1, turn.

Row 5: Dc in all sts, ch1, turn. (28 dc)

Row 6: Dc2tog, dc in next 24 sts, dc2tog, ch1, turn.

Row 7: Dc in all sts, ch1, turn. (26 dc)

Row 8: Dc2tog, dc in next 22 sts, dc2tog, ch1, turn.

Row 9: Dc in all sts, ch1, turn. (24 dc)
Continue decreasing on all the even rows and working the odd rows in dc.

See small triangle for fastening off.

Block all triangles.

Assembly and finishing

Front

Sew small triangles together on the reverse with a slip stitch to form a large triangle.

Weave in ends.

Front layout

Using the main colour and front facing, attach the front to the back with a double crochet join putting 3dc at each corner.

Stuff with hollowfibre filling as the third side is completed, paying particular attention to each corner.

Fasten off and weave ends in the reverse side.

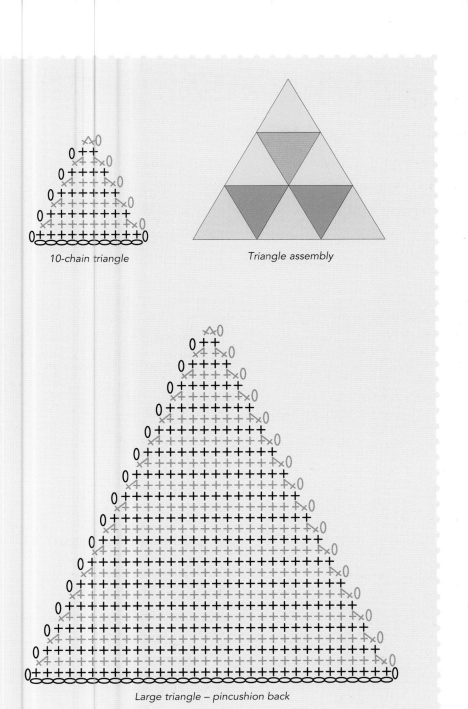

10-chain triangle

Triangle assembly

Large triangle – pincushion back

Polka Dots

This is an easy introduction to intarsia. Each cream dot is worked separately so there's no messy carrying over of yarn. Add ribbon and matching polka dot buttons for a fun finish to your pincushion.

SKILL LEVEL

Tools & Materials

DK wool:

A pink: 7.75m (8½yds)

B blue: 7.75m (8½yds)

C cream (also used for dots C):
9.25m (10yds)

Knitting needles: 2.75mm
(US size 2)

1 polka dot button

Narrow ribbon

Hollowfibre filling

Front

Using A, cast on 17 sts.

Row 1: Knit.

Row 2: Purl.

Row 3: K4A, k1C, k7A, k1C, k4A.

Row 4: P3A, p3C, p5A, p3C, p3A.

Row 5: K3A, k3C, k5A, k3C, k3A.

Row 6: P4A, p1C, p3A, p1C, p3A, p1C, p4A.

Row 7: K7A, k3C, k7A.

Row 8: P7A, p3C, p7A.

Row 9: K8A, k1C, k8A.

Row 10: Purl in A.

Substituting A with B, rep first 10 rows.

Break off B.

Using C only, work 10 rows in st st.

Cast off.

Back

Using A, cast on 17 sts.

Work 10 rows in st st.

Change to B.

Work 10 rows in st st.

Change to C.

Work 10 rows in st st.

Cast off.

Assembly and finishing

Weave in all ends and block.

Attach front to back, adding stuffing as you sew up the fourth side.

Sew the ribbon around the pincushion with a slip stitch, fastening at the back. Sew on the button.

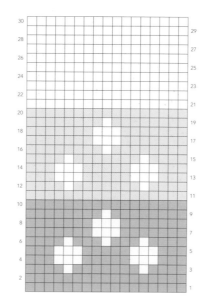

Seed Pearls

This is a perfect introduction to embellishing with beads. The combination of soft oyster pink yarn and seed pearls produces a delicate pincushion.

Front

Thread 24 beads on to yarn before starting.

Cast on 18 sts.

Row 1: Knit.

Row 2: Purl.

Row 3: Knit.

Row 4: Purl.

Row 5: K1, (yo, slip 1, pb, k1, psso) to last st, k1.

Row 6: Purl.

Rep first 6 rows twice. Work 6 rows st st beg with a k row. Cast off knitwise.

Back

Cast on 18 sts.

Beg with a k row, work rows in sl st until back measures the same as front.

Cast off knitwise.

Eyelet edging strip

Cast on 5 sts.

Row 1: Knit.

Row 2: Purl.

Row 3: K2, yo, skpo, k1.

Row 4: Purl.

These 4 rows form the pattern. Rep until strip measures around the four sides of the pincushion.

Keep sts on the needle so that when the edging is sewn in place, you can work a couple of extra rows if needed.

Assembly and finishing

Before sewing the edging in place, thread beads on the ribbon and weave the ribbon through the eyelets, making sure the ribbon is threading correctly to tie in place.

Slipstitch the felt to the wrong side of the front; this will prevent the stuffing from coming through the pincushion front. Sew edging to the front. When nearing the end, cast off the stitches on the edging and sew both ends together.

Sew the edging to the back, stuffing before finishing the fourth side.

Spot stitch pearl beads around the top edge to correspond with the beads that have been knitted in.

Tie the ribbon into a bow at the front.

Handy hint

Thread the beads on at the working end of the yarn before casting on. Slide each bead in place on Row 5.

SKILL LEVEL

Tools & Materials

Soft pink DK wool:
30.25m (33yds)

Knitting needles: 2.75mm (US size 2)

Toning felt for containing the stuffing

Seed pearl beads (approx 50)

Oyster ribbon

Hollowfibre filling

Special abbreviation

pb = place bead – bring yarn to front of work, slip 1, slide 1 bead up yarn ready to be worked, k1, add a bead so that it is facing the front on the knit stitch, pass the slip stitch over the bead to hold it in place.

Cupcake

Who can resist a cupcake? This pincushion is strawberry flavored with a golden brown cake base. Topped with a swirl of cream and a cherry on top, it's good enough to eat.

SKILL LEVEL

Tools & Materials

DK cotton:

Brown: 18.5m (20yds)

Pink: 10m (11yds)

Cream: 9.25m (10yds)

Mercerised cotton:

Red: 2.75m (3yds)

Green: 2.25m (2½yds)

Crochet hook: 3.5mm (US size E) and 2.75mm (US size C)

Hollowfibre filling

Foam for base

Base

Use a stitch marker in first st in each rnd. Using brown and 3.5mm (US size E) hook:

Foundation round: Ch2, 6dc in second st from hook. (6 dc)

Round 2: 2dc in each st. (12 dc)

Round 3: (Dc in next st, 2dc in next st) 6 times. (18 dc)

Round 4: (Dc in next 2 sts, 2dc in next st) 6 times. (24 dc)

Round 5: (Dc in next 3 sts, 2dc in next st) 6 times. (30 dc)

Round 6: (Dc in next 4 sts, 2dc in next st) 6 times. (36 dc)

Fasten off.

Side

Using brown and 3.5mm (US size E) hook:

Foundation row: Ch10, dc in second st from hook, dc in each ch, ch1, turn.

Row 1: Front post dc in all sts, ch1, turn.

Row 2: Dc in all sts, ch1, turn.

Rep Rows 1–2 until the side measures the same as the perimeter of the base.

Top

Using pink and 3.5mm (US size E) hook:

Foundation round: Ch2, 6dc in second st from hook. (6 dc)

Working in the back loop only of all sts, work as follows:

Round 2: 2dc in each st. (12 dc)

Round 3: (Dc in next st, 2dc in next st) 6 times, mark this place with a stitch marker. (18 dc)

Round 4: (Dc in next 2 sts, 2dc in next st) 6 times. (24 dc)

Round 5: (Dc in next 3 sts, 2dc in next st) 6 times. (30 dc)

Round 6: (Dc in next 4 sts, 2dc in next st) 6 times. (36 dc)

Round 7: Dc in all sts.

Round 8: Dc in all sts, ch1, turn.

Do not break yarn.

Icing top stitching: With pink slip st in front loop of all sts to marker placed on Rnd 3.

Change to cream.

Working into front loop only of rem sts, (htr, tr, htr) in each st until the first round, then (htr, tr, htr) into the side of sts in first rnd.

Fasten off.

Cherry

Using red and 2.75mm (US size C) hook:

Foundation round: Ch2, 6dc in second st from hook. (6 dc)

Round 2: 2dc in each st. (12 dc)

Round 3: (Dc in next st, 2dc in next st) 6 times. (18 dc)

Round 4: Dc in all sts.

Round 5: (Dc2tog) 6 times.

Stuff with hollowfibre filling.

Round 6: (Dc2tog) 3 times.

Gather sts to close.

Stem

Using green and 2.75mm (US size C) hook, ch10, slip st in each ch, fasten off.

Leaf

The leaf is worked around the first 7 chain sts.

Using green and 2.75mm (US size C) hook, ch7.

Working through top loops of chs, slip st

to top loop of second st from hook, dc, htr, tr, htr, 2dc in first ch, then working up other side of chs work htr, tr, htr, dc, slip st to first slip st.

Fasten off leaving a tail for sewing.

Assembly and finishing

With a blunt-ended needle, attach base to side before joining the back seam.

Sew the stem and leaf to the cherry and attach to top of cupcake.

Weave in ends to the reverse.

Insert foam into the base and stuff with hollowfibre filling.

Pin the top of the cupcake to the sides.

Join cream yarn to the seam and attach the top to the side.

Cream edging

With top of cupcake facing, ch2, tr, htr in same st, (dc in next st, htr, tr, htr in next st) around, slip st to first ch.

You might have to adjust the sts as you ease the sides in.

Make sure the cake is fully stuffed before finishing off the join.

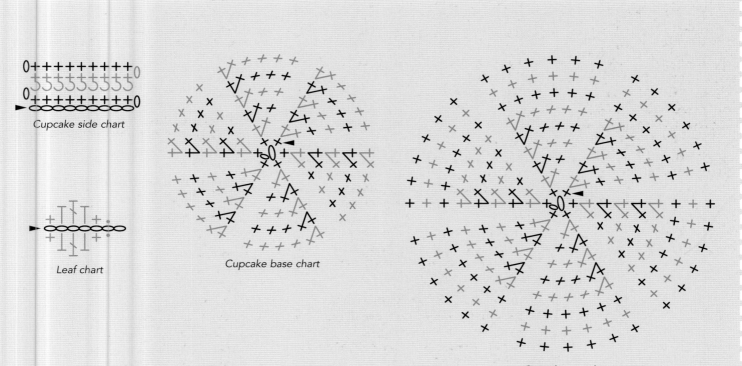

Cupcake side chart

Leaf chart

Cupcake base chart

Cupcake top chart

From the Vine

This fruity twist on a traditional pineapple motif resembles a bunch of grapes. Choose either variety: green or purple. It's quick to make, leaving you plenty of time to enjoy a glass of Chardonnay or Merlot later.

SKILL LEVEL

Tools & Materials
Mercerised crochet thread:
38m (41yds)
Crochet hook: 3mm (US size C/D)
Cotton fabric for cushion pad
Hollowfibre filling

Front and back

Row 1: Ch5 (includes first dtr), 10dtr in first ch. (11 dtr)

Row 2: Ch4 (includes first tr and ch-1 sp), tr in next st, (ch1, tr) to end of row, ch1, turn.

Row 3: Slip st in first space, ch3, 4tr in same space, pull yarn from front of top on ch3 (beginning popcorn), (ch1, popcorn in next ch-1 sp) to end, ch1, turn.

Row 4: Slip st in first ch-1 sp, (ch3, slip st in next ch sp) to end, ch1, turn.

Row 5: Slip st in first space, ch3, 4tr in same ch-3 sp, pull yarn from front of top on ch3 (beginning popcorn), (ch1, popcorn in next ch-3 sp) to end, ch1, turn.

Rep Rows 4 and 5 three times.

There should be two popcorns in the last row.

Do not turn on the final row. The working loop will start the join. Leave this loop loose on the front to pick up for the join.

Side loops

On back only work down the left-hand side ch3, slip st to the base of the next popcorn. Rep to the first popcorn row, ch3, slip st in side of dtr, ch3, slip st in first ch, ch3, slip st in side of the first tr on the opposite side, rep ch3, slip st as for first side, placing final slip st between the two popcorns in last row. Fasten off.

Stalk

Make a chain 7.5cm (3in) long. Skip 1ch, slip st in each ch.

Fasten off.

Assembly and finishing

Pad

Use the motif as a template for the cushion pad. Cut out two pieces of cotton plus extra for the seam allowance. Stitch, leaving a gap to stuff with hollowfibre filling. Turn the right way, stuff and finish with a slip stitch.

Place the front and back motifs together with WS facing. Insert the hook into the working loop and attach.

Ch1, dc into corresponding ch3 loop on the back, ch1, slip st to base of next popcorn. Rep this around the motif placing the slip st in exactly the same position as the back.

Insert the pad before the second side is completed. Fasten off and weave in ends.

Ammonite

This spiral motif gives you the chance to experience freeform crochet. Instructions are given for the start, but then the choice is yours. Pick your own stitches and increases for an individual look.

Spiral motif

Unlike most rounds there is no join. The colours literally spiral around each other. All stitches are worked in the back loop of the previous round.

Marking the first and last st in each round will help keep count.

Begin with a sliding loop.

Round 1: Using cream, work 10sc in loop.

Round 2: Using gun grey metallic yarn, join in sliding loop behind cream, dc in sliding loop, dc in back loop of all dc of first rnd.

Round 3: Join in blue in sliding loop behind grey, dc in sliding loop, dc in back loop of all dc of Rnd 2.

Round 4: Join in coral in sliding loop behind blue, dc in sliding loop, dc in back loop of all dc of Rnd 3.

Pull loop shut.

These four rounds begin the spiral. You can now decide which colours to increase. The amount of increases in the rows will depend on how the motif lies. If it starts to cup, work more increases in the round. If it ruffles, work fewer increases.

The instructions are a guide to the increases if cream is worked as tr and blue is worked as htr, changing to tr in the final round. Grey and coral are worked as dc.

Second spiral is a continuation of first rnd.

Mark first and last st in the rnds.

Round 1: Dc in next 5 sts, htr in next 4 sts, 2tr in each st to end.

Round 2: Dc in all sts.

Round 3: Dc in next 5 sts, 2htr in each st to end.

Round 4: Dc in all sts.

Third spiral

Round 1: (2tr in next st, tr) to marker.

Round 2: Dc in each st.

Round 3: (2tr in next st, tr) to marker.

Round 4: Dc in each st.

Decide how large you want to make your pincushion and finish at any point making sure that all colours are worked to the same place.

Assembly and finishing

The shape of the spiral means that if you make the back the same as the front, it will have to be reversed when sewing it up. It depends how neat your reverse work is. If you go with this option, the ends on the back will need to be woven in the right side of your work.

Attach with a double crochet join in the last colour used in the spiral.

Alternatively, contrasting material can be sewn to the reverse of the spiral. Use the spiral as a template for your cushion (see page 17 for 'fabric inserts'). Add extra for a seam allowance before cutting out your material. Stuff with hollowfibre filling. Sew to the front with a slip stitch.

SKILL LEVEL

Tools & Materials

4-ply yarn:

Cream: 4m (4½yds)

Gun grey metallic yarn: 2.75m (3yds)

Blue: 4m (4½yds)

Coral: 3.75m (4yds)

Crochet hook: 2.5mm (US size B/C)

Stitch markers

Choice of backing – either the reverse of the motif or contrasting cotton

Hollowfibre filling

Beginning of the spiral

Dala Horse

The traditional wooden Dala horse was first carved to serve as a children's toy. Knit it in the original red colour for the authentic Swedish look.

SKILL LEVEL

Tools & Materials

DK wool:
A cream: 27.5m (30yds)
B red: 6.5m (7yds)
Knitting needles: 3mm (US size 2/3)
Hollowfibre filling

Front

Using A cast on 24 sts.

Row 1: K2A, k1B, k4A, k1B, k1A, k1B, k4A, k1B, k4A, k1B, k1A, k1B, k2A.

Row 2: (P1A, p2B, p1A, p2B, p2A, p1B, p1A, p1B, p1A) twice.

Row 3: K1B, k3A, k2B, k2A, k1B, k2A, k2B, k3A, k2B, k2A, k1B, k2A, k1B.

Row 4: As Row 2.

Row 5: As Row 1.

Break off B.

Row 6: Purl.

Row 7: Knit.

Rejoin B.

Row 8: P5A, p3B, p5A, p3B, p8A.

Row 9: K8A, k3B, k5A, k3B, k5A.

Row 10: As Row 8.

Row 11: As Row 9.

Row 12: As Row 8.

Row 13: K8A, k5B, k1A, k5B, k5A.

Row 14: P5A, p5B, p1A, p5B, p8A.

Row 15: K8A, k3B, k5A, k3B, k5A.

Row 16: P5A, p3B, p1A, p3B, p1A, p3B, p8A.

Row 17: K8A, k3B, k1A, k3B, k1A, k3B, k5A.

Row 18: P6A, p2B, p1A, p3B, p1A, p3B, p1A, p3B, p4A.

Row 19: K4A, k7B, k1A, k1B, k11A.

Row 20: P13A, p6B, p5A.

Row 21: K5A, k5B, k14A.

Row 22: P15A, p3B, p6A.

Row 23: K6A, k1B, k17A.

Break off B.

Row 24: Purl in A.

Repeat rows 1–6.

Cast off.

Back

Using A only, cast on 24 sts. Beg with a k row work in st st for 30 rows. Cast off.

Assembly and finishing

Weave in all ends. Block the front.

Sew the front to the back adding stuffing as you go. Pay particular attention to the corners.

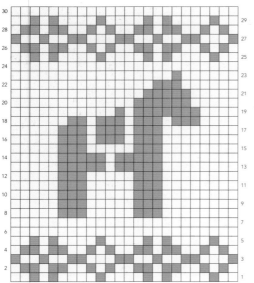

Pocketful of Lace

Worked in the traditional feather and fan stitch, this dainty pincushion is fastened with three mother-of-pearl buttons. By using a fine needle and 4-ply yarn, an airy lacy finish is created. Make it more precious by adding a rosette flower.

Pocket

Using lavender cast on 36 sts.

Row 1: Knit.

Row 2: Purl.

Row 3: *K2tog 3 times, (yo, k1) 6 times, k2tog 3 times, rep from * once.

Row 4: Knit.

These four rows form the pattern. Repeat until work measures the desired length. Cast off.

Rosette

Using pink, cast on 8 sts.

Row 1: K1, (yo, k1) until end of row.

Row 2: Purl.

Row 3: Knit.

Row 4: Cast off purlwise.

Assembly and finishing

Fold over work with an overlap for the buttons. Sew the side seams only with a slip stitch.

Sew the buttons in place.

Gather the rosette together and sew in place. Add a seed pearl bead to the centre.

Cut fabric into two rectangles to measurement of pocket plus 12mm (½in) seam allowance all round.

With WS of fabric together either machine stitch or back stitch around 3 sides using a 12mm (½in) seam allowance.

Turn cushion right side out and stuff with cotton wadding. Sew up fourth side of insert using ladder stitch.

SKILL LEVEL

Tools & Materials

4-ply merino wool:

Lavender: 58.5m (64yds)

Pink: 1m (1yd)

Knitting needles: 2mm (US size 0)

3 buttons

1 seed pearl bead

Contrasting fabric for insert

Cotton wadding for filling

An Arrangement

Why not organise your work with a pincushion that doubles as a wall hanging? The square pockets are ideal for holding scissors, thimble and threads. Add in the handy measuring tape ribbon for instant reference.

SKILL LEVEL

Tools & Materials

DK mercerised cotton:

Main section

Aqua: 127m (140yds)

Pockets

A blue: 1m (1yd)

B pink: 2.3m (2½yds)

C lime green: 3.8m (4⅛yds)

Crochet hook: 3mm (US size D)

15cm (6in) embroidery hoop

10cm (4in) ribbon tape

2 buttons

Cotton wadding

Thin cork

Twine for hanging

Front

Make two circles. The front will need to be larger to allow for an overlap. When working the increases the 2dc should always be worked in the V shape formed by the increase in the previous row.

Begin with sliding loop.

Round 1: Slip st, ch3 (counts a first tr), 11dc, slip st to top of ch3, pull loop shut. (12 tr)

Round 2: Ch3, tr in same st, (2tr in next st) 11 times, slip st to top of ch3. (24 tr)

Round 3: Ch3, 2tr in next st, (tr in next st, 2tr in next st) 11 times, slip st to top of ch3. (36 tr)

Round 4: Ch3, tr in next st, 2tr in next st, (tr in next 2 sts, 2tr in next st) 11 times, slip st to top of ch3. (48 tr)

Round 5: Ch3, tr in next 2 sts, 2tr in next st, (tr in next 3 sts, 2tr in next st) 11 times, slip st to top of ch3. (60 tr)

Round 6: Ch3, tr in next 3 sts, 2tr in next st, (tr in next 4 sts, 2tr in next st) 11 times, slip st to top of ch3. (72 tr)

Continue increasing until the circle measures 15cm (6in).

Once you have reached the 15cm (6in) diameter needed, stop increasing and work in treble crochet for two rounds. This allows your circle to cup, enabling you to fix your circle in the hoop with an overlap.

Fasten off and weave in ends.

Back

Work as for front, but once you have reached the 15cm (6in) diameter, stop increasing. Fasten off leaving a long tail for sewing. Weave in the circle's centre end.

Pockets

For the large pocket make a simple square using three colours. For the small pocket complete the first two rows only using two colours.

Large pocket

Simple square (three rounds).

Foundation row: Using yarn A begin with ch5, join to first ch with a slip st to form a ring.

Round 1: In ring ch3 (counts as first tr), 2tr, (ch2, 3tr in ring) 3 times, ch2, slip st to top of ch3. (3 tr each side)

Round 2: Change to yarn B, join in any of 2ch spaces, ch3, tr in space, tr in next 3 sts, 2tr in ch2 space, (ch2, 2tr in same ch2 space, tr in next 3 sts, 2tr in next ch2 space) 3 times, ch2, slip st to top of ch3. (7 tr each side)

Round 3: Change to yarn C, join in any of 2ch spaces, ch3, tr in same space, tr in next 7 sts, 2tr in ch2 space, (ch2, 2tr in same ch2 space, tr in next 7 sts, 2tr in ch2 space) 3 times, ch2, slip st to top of ch3 to complete the round. (11 tr each side)

Fasten off leaving a long tail for sewing.

Weave in all ends.

For the small pocket make two rounds of the simple square.

Assembly and finishing

Pin the pockets in position on the front and sew in place, leaving the top of the pockets open.

Pin the tape in position and sew in place with a slip stitch.

Sew a button at either end of the tape.

Fix the front inside the hoop making sure that the screw is at the top. Tighten the screw so that the hoop holds in place.

Cut 15cm (6in) diameter layers of cotton wadding to fit inside the ring so that the front lies flat. This can be held in place at the back with a thin circle of cork cut to size.

With the back piece face up, place it over the cork and stitch to the front piece with a slip stitch.

Double over the twine and tie around the screw to make a loop for hanging.

Basic 12-stitch circle

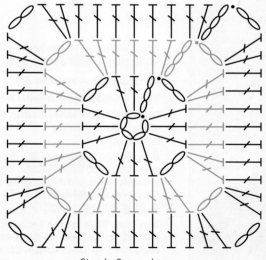

Simple 3-round square

Birdhouse

This pincushion is not only pretty, but functional too. You can organise your equipment with the clever use of perches. Add dowel rods to attach your threads and tools and have everything at hand to complete your projects.

Birdhouse – make two

Using cream, cast on 18 sts.

Row 1: Knit.

Row 2: Purl.

These 2 rows form st st.

Work in st st for 5cm (2in).

Next row: Cast on 3 sts, k to end.

Next row: Cast on 3 sts, p to end.

Decrease rows

Next row: Skpo, k to last 2 sts, k2tog.

Next row: Purl.

Rep last 2 rows until 4 sts rem.

Next row: Skpo, k2tog.

Next row: K2tog.

Fasten off.

Side

Using cream, cast on 6 sts.

Work in st st until piece is long enough to measure all around the birdhouse.

Do not cast off until work is sewn up, just in case extra length is needed.

Front – make one

Using green, cast on 14 sts.

Row 1: Knit.

Row 2: Slip 1, purl to end.

Row 3: Slip 1, knit to end.

Cont in st st, slipping the first st in each row for a neat edge until work measures 5cm (2in).

Decrease rows

Next row: Skpo, k to last 2 sts, k2tog.

Next row: Purl.

Rep last 2 rows until 4 sts rem.

Next row: Skpo, k2tog.

Next row: K2tog.

Fasten off.

Assembly and finishing

Sew buttons to the front before sewing the front piece to the top of the birdhouse.

Sew the side piece to the top working extra rows if necessary.

Cut the foam to fit the shape of the birdhouse. Place foam in birdhouse then sew bottom of birdhouse to side piece.

Sand down one end of the dowels. Sharpen the other ends of the dowel to a point.

Poke the dowel through it into the foam. The dowel can be glued into place. When the dowel is stuck firmly sew the side to the back.

Wrap green wool around the grips of the scissors and oversew to fasten in place.

Make a hanging loop with the twine and decorate with a bow. Tie a loop of twine around the scissors. These can then be balanced on the perches.

Button Stripes

The starting point for this pincushion was a charming handmade ceramic button. From there, just pick your favourite colours and match the yarn. Add a simple garter stitch frill for extra flounce.

Front and back – make two

Using 3.5mm (US size 9/10) needles and red, cast on 22 sts.

Row 1: Knit.

Row 2: Purl.

These 2 rows set st st.

Work 2 more rows in red.

Fasten off red and join in cream.

Joining in colours as they appear and carrying cream yarn up the ends of the rows without fastening off, cont as follows:

Work 2 rows in cream.

Work 2 rows in fuchsia.

Work 2 rows in cream.

Work 2 rows in pink.

Work 2 rows in cream.

Work 2 rows in lilac.

Work 2 rows in cream.

Work 2 rows in blue.

Work 2 rows in cream.

Work 2 rows in dark blue.

Work 2 rows in cream.

Work 4 rows in green.

Cast off.

Garter stitch bow

Using 2.75mm (US size 2) needles and cream, cast on 12 sts.

Knit 14 rows.

Cast off.

Using cream wool wrap around the centre to pinch halves together. This yarn can then be used to sew the bow in place.

Frill

Using 2.75mm (US size 2) needles and cream, cast on 4 stitches.

Row 1: Knit.

Row 2: Slip 1, k to end.

Rep last row until work measures at least two and a half times the distance around the pincushion. Leave the working sts on a stitch holder until the frill has been sewn in place in case you need to knit extra rows.

Assembly and finishing

Attach front to back, stuffing as you work the fourth side. Pay particular attention to the corners.

Sew the bow to the front. Sew the button to the bow.

Join cream thread to end edge of the frill. Work a running stitch to the end. Gather up the frill and stitch to the outside seam.

SKILL LEVEL

Tools & Materials

DK wool:

Red: 3.75m (4yds)

Cream: 47.5m (52yds)

Fuchsia: 1.75m (2yds)

Pink: 1.75m (2yds)

Lilac: 1.75m (2yds)

Blue: 1.75m (2yds)

Dark blue: 1.75m (2yds)

Green: 3.75m (4yds)

Knitting needles: 2.75mm (US size 2) and 3.5mm (US size 9/10)

1 striped button

Hollowfibre filling

Fuchsia

This pretty pink pincushion features a fold-down buttonhole band with vintage buttons. This means the pad can be swapped around if you want to change the colours peeking through the openwork mesh.

SKILL LEVEL

Tools & Materials
Pink DK mercerised cotton:
51m (55yds)
3 small buttons
Crochet hook: 2.75mm (US size C)
Hollowfibre filling
Cotton fabric for insert
Sewing thread and needle

Work rounds 1–5 for both sides. The front has one row of button band while the back has three rows of buttonhole band.

Front
Begin with a sliding loop.

Round 1: Slip st, ch3 (counts as first tr), 2tr in ring, (ch3, 3tr in ring) 3 times, ch1, htr to top of ch3, pull loop shut. (3tr each side)

Round 2: Ch3, tr in space formed by htr, tr in top of ch3 used to make the htr, tr in next 2 sts, 2tr in ch3 space, (ch3, 2tr in the space, tr in next 3 sts, 2tr in next space) 3 times, ch1, htr to top of ch3. (7 tr on each side)

Round 3: Ch4 (counts as first tr and ch1 space), tr in top of ch3 used to make the htr, (ch1, skip 1, tr in next st) 3 times, ch1, tr in ch3 space, *ch3, tr in ch3 space, (ch1, skip 1, tr in next st) 4 times, ch1, tr in ch3 space*, repeat from * to * 2 more times, ch1, htr to top of ch3. (6 tr each side)

Round 4: Ch3, tr in space formed by the htr, tr in top of ch3 used to make htr, tr in next 10 sts, 2tr in ch3 space, (ch3, 2tr in ch3 space, tr in next 11 sts, 2tr in ch3 space) 3 times, ch1, htr to top of ch3. (15 tr each side)

Round 5: Ch3, tr in space formed by the htr, tr in top of ch3 used to make htr, tr in next 14 sts, 2tr in ch3 space, (ch3, 2tr in ch3 space, tr in next 15 sts, 2tr in ch3 space) 3 times, ch1, htr to top of ch3. (19 tr each side)

Front button band
Row 1: Ch3 (counts as first tr), tr in space formed by the htr, tr in top of ch3 used to make htr, tr in next 18 sts, 2tr in ch3 space, fasten off. (23 tr)

Back buttonhole band
Row 1: Ch3 (counts as first tr), tr in space formed by the htr, tr in top of ch3 used to make htr, tr in next 18 sts, 2tr in ch3 space, ch3, turn. (23 tr)

Row 2: Tr in each st across row, ch3, turn.

Row 3: Tr in each st across row.

Fasten off and weave in the ends.

Block before joining.

Assembly and finishing
Place front and back together so that button bands are at the top and leave open. With wrong sides together, work a double crochet join with 3dc in the corners for a neat turn. Sew three buttons on the front button band.

Insert the stuffed casing (see page 17 for 'fabric inserts'). Fold over the buttonhole band and fasten the buttons in the spaces between treble crochets.

Weave in all ends.

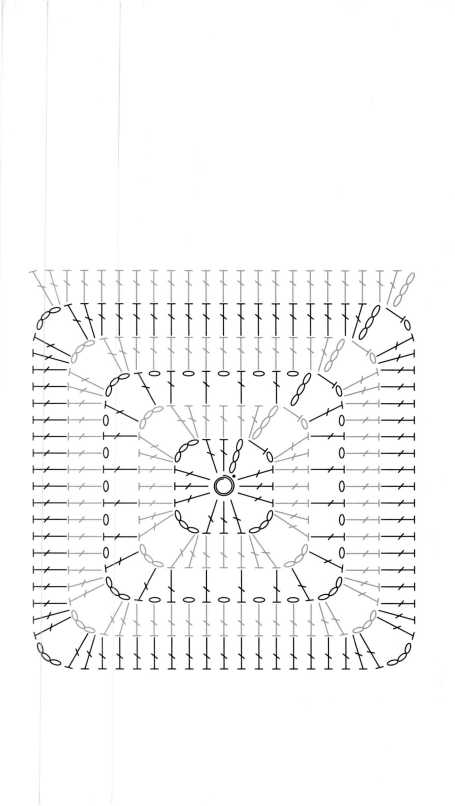

Spike the Cactus

Spike the cactus is, without doubt, one of the easiest pincushions to make. It is a pain-free introduction to knitting with beads. Simply work the pieces as rectangles and sew into tubes. Finish with a tiny flower button.

SKILL LEVEL

Tools & Materials

DK wool:

A green and yellow twist: 12.5m (13½yds)

B terracotta: 25.5m (28yds)

Pink: 41cm (16in)

Knitting needles: 3mm (US size 2/3)

Yellow sewing thread

Shallow dish or ramekin

Gilt beads

Small yellow flower button

Hollowfibre filling

Special abbreviation

pb = place bead

Pre-string the beads on to the yarn. Slide the bead up the yarn and place close to the needle as you knit the stitch.

Main stem

Using A, cast on 24 sts.

Row 1: Knit.

Row 2: Purl.

Row 3: Knit.

Row 4: K5, pb, k4, pb, (k3, pb) twice, k to end.

Row 5: Knit.

Row 6: Purl.

Row 7: Knit.

Row 8: K7, pb, k3, pb, k4, pb, k to end.

Rep these 8 rows three more times.

Cast off.

Side stems

Using A cast on 15 sts.

Row 1: Knit.

Row 2: Purl.

Row 3: Knit.

Row 4: (K3, pb) 3 times, k to end.

Row 5: Knit.

Row 6: Purl.

Row 7: Knit.

Row 8: K4, pb, (k3, pb) twice, k to end.

Rep these 8 rows twice more.

Cast off.

Pot

Measure the depth of the bowl. The work will need to cover it from the centre of the inside to the centre of the base. Cast on enough stitches to measure this distance. A trial tension square will help to work this out.

Knit a strip in garter stitch (every row knit) to go around the outside when slightly stretched.

Assembly and finishing

Cactus (all pieces the same)

Sew the cast-on and cast-off edges together. Sew running sts on one side edge and gather together tightly. Stuff with hollowfibre filling.

Sew the shorter pieces to the side of the main stem.

Knot short pieces of sewing thread around some of the beads for spikes.

Flower

Cut four short pieces of pink wool. Knot these through the top of the main stem and sew the flower button in the centre. Unravel the yarn to make the flower fuller.

Bowl

Sew the cast-on and cast-off edges of the strip together. Sew running sts on both side edges. Gather one side together and place the bowl inside and stuff. Gather the other side together.

Firmly sew the base of the cactus stem in place on the bowl.

Pear

This is a sweet, fruity pincushion that is knitted in the round. The Aran-weight yarn and no seaming means that it knits up quickly. Top with a stalk and a leaf or two for a pincushion that will look great in your kitchen fruit bowl.

Pear

Using green Aran yarn and 4mm (US size 6) knitting needles, cast on 4 sts and divide over three needles. Mark first stitch on each row.

Row 1: Knit, starting with the first st on the left-hand needle. Pull the first stitch tightly to avoid making a gap.

Row 2: Kfb in each st. (8 sts)

Row 3: Knit.

Row 4: Kfb in each st. (16 sts)

Row 5: Knit.

Row 6: Kfb in each st. (32 sts)

Rows 7–12: Knit.

Row 13: (K1, k2tog) to last 2 sts, k2tog. (21 sts)

Row 14: Knit.

Row 15: (K1, k2tog) to end. (14 sts)

Row 16: Knit.

Row 17: (K1, k2tog) to last 2 sts, k2tog. (9 sts)

Rows 18–24: Knit.

Row 25: (K1, k2tog) to end. (6 sts)

Thread yarn through rem sts.

Leaf

Using green and 3mm (US size 2/3) knitting needles, cast on 3 sts.

Row 1: Knit.

Row 2: Purl.

Row 3: Kfb, k1, m1b, k1. (5 sts)

Row 4: Purl.

Row 5: Skpo, k1, k2tog. (3 sts)

Row 6: Purl.

Row 7: Sk2po.

Fasten off.

Stalk

Using brown and 2.5mm (US size 1/2) double-pointed needles, cast on 2 sts and make an i-cord as follows:

Row 1: Knit, slide sts to other end of needle, keep thread behind the work ready to knit next row.

Rep this row for 2.5cm (1in).

Cast off.

Assembly and finishing

Stuff the pear before pulling the yarn tight.

Sometimes knitters new to using double-pointed needles may not pull the yarn tightly enough when working the change of needles. If this has happened and gaps have appeared, use an unsewn tube of toning felt as a casing for the stuffing.

Sew the stem and leaf in place before weaving in the ends.

SKILL LEVEL

Tools & Materials

Aran wool:

Green: 9.25m (10yds)

DK wool:

Dark green: 45.75cm (18in)

Brown: 45.75cm (18in)

Knitting needles:

3mm (US size 2/3) straight needles

Set of four 4mm (US size 6) double-pointed needles

Two 2.5mm (US size 1/2) double-pointed needles

Hollowfibre filling

Yellow felt – optional

Circus Time

Add circus flair to your craft table. Combining triangles and octagons, this pincushion also has an appliqué star for a fairground feel.

SKILL LEVEL

Tools & Materials

DK mercerised cotton:
Blue: 25.5m (28yds)
Green: 15.25m (18⅓yds)
Red: 10.75m (11½yds)
Cream: 2.5m (100in)
Crochet hook: 2.75mm (US size C)
2 foam pieces, 2.5cm (1in) thick,
to match the finished shape

Green triangles

Make six 10-chain triangles.

Row 1: Ch11, dc in second st from hook, dc in all sts, ch1, turn. (10 dc)

Row 2: Dc2tog, dc in next 6 sts, dc2tog, ch1, turn.

Row 3: Dc in all sts, ch1, turn. (8 dc)

Row 4: Dc2tog, dc in next 4 sts, dc2tog, ch1, turn.

Row 5: Dc in all sts, ch1, turn. (6 dc)

Row 6: Dc2tog, dc in next 2 sts, dc2tog, ch1, turn.

Row 7: Dc in all sts, ch1, turn. (4 dc)

Row 8: Dc2tog twice, ch1, turn.

Row 9: Dc in both sts, ch1, turn. (2 dc)

Row 10: Dc2tog.

Fasten off leaving a tail for sewing in.

Red triangles

Make six 8-chain triangles.

Row 1: Ch9, dc in second st from hook, dc in all sts, ch1, turn. (8 dc)

Row 2: Dc2tog, dc in next 4 sts, dc2tog, ch1, turn.

Row 3: Dc in all sts, ch1, turn. (6 dc)

Row 4 Dc2tog, dc in next 2 sts, dc2tog, ch1, turn.

Row 5: Dc in all sts, ch1, turn. (4 dc)

Row 6: Dc2tog twice, ch1, turn.

Row 7: Dc in both sts, ch1, turn. (2 dc)

Row 8: Dc2tog.

Fasten off leaving a tail for sewing in.

Hexagon base

Begin with a sliding loop.

Round 1: Slip st, ch3 (counts as first tr), 11dc in ring, slip st to top of ch3, pull loop shut. (12 tr)

Round 2: Ch3, 3tr in next st, (tr in next st, 3tr in next st) 5 times, slip st to top of ch3. (24 tr)

Round 3: Ch3, tr in next st, 3tr in next st, (tr in next 3 sts, 3tr in next st) 5 times, tr in next st, slip st to top of ch3. (36 tr)

Round 4: Ch3, tr in next 2 sts, 3tr in next st, (tr in next 5 sts, 3tr in next st) 5 times, tr in next 2 sts, slip st to top of ch3. (48 tr)

Round 5: Ch3, tr in next 3 sts, 3tr in next st, (tr in next 7 sts, 3tr in next st) 5 times, tr in next 3 sts, slip st to top of ch3. (60 tr)

Hexagon top

Begin with a sliding loop.

Round 1: Slip st, ch3 (counts as first tr), 11dc in ring, slip st to top of ch3, pull loop shut. (12 tr)

Round 2: Ch3, 3tr in next st, (tr in next st, 3tr in next st) 5 times, slip st to top of ch3. (24 tr)

Round 3: Ch3, 1tr in next st, 3tr in next st, (tr in next 3 sts, 3tr in next st) 5 times, tr in next st, slip st to top of ch3. (36 tr)

Round 4: (Worked in exactly the same way as base Round 4 but substituting tr for htr): ch2 (counts as first htr), htr in next 2 sts, 3htr in next st, (htr in next 5 sts, 3htr in next st) 5 times, htr in next 2 sts, slip st to top of ch3. (48 htr)

Star

Begin with a sliding loop.

Round 1: Slip st, dc, (tr, picot3, tr, dc) 4 times, tr, picot3, tr, in the ring, slip st to first ch, pull loop shut.

Fasten off leaving a long tail for sewing to the top.

Assembly and finishing

Sew the star to the top.

With the top facing, attach to the base of the red triangles using a double crochet join. The corners of the triangles should meet the corners of the hexagon top.

Sew a cream cross stitch star on each green triangle.

Attach the first two rows of the green triangles together starting at the base before joining to the red triangle with a backstitch on the reverse. This forms the sides of the shape.

Weave in all loose ends.

Cut the foam to match the size of the shape. Depending on the depth of the sides you might need two pieces. These can be tapered so that they are narrower at the top.

Insert the foam. Pin the base to the side section matching the corners of the hexagon to the triangle joins. Attach the base to the green triangles using a double crochet join.

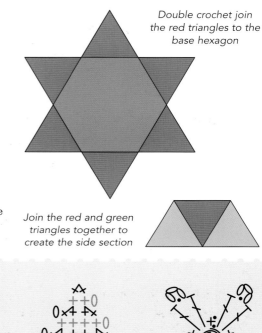

Double crochet join the red triangles to the base hexagon

Join the red and green triangles together to create the side section

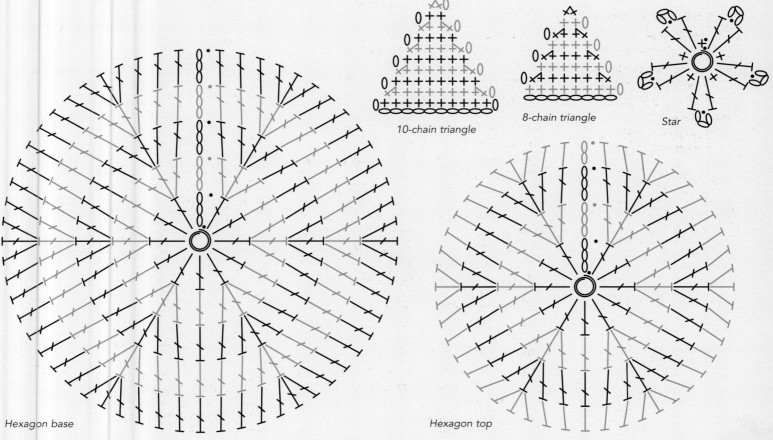

10-chain triangle

8-chain triangle

Star

Hexagon base

Hexagon top

Flower Power

This is an easy way to keep your pins at hand.
Simply place around your wrist and fasten with a toggle.
The length of the strap can be easily adjusted to fit.

SKILL LEVEL

Tools & Materials

4-ply cotton:

Green: 5m (5½yds)
Pink: 6.5m (7yds)
Purple: 16.5m (18yds)
Crochet hook: 2.5mm (US size C)
1 polka dot button
1 toggle button
Hollowfibre filling

Flower

Using green, work as follows:

Foundation round: Ch2, 6dc in second st from hook. (6 dc)

Round 2: 2dc in each st. (12 dc)

Round 3: (Dc, 2dc in next st) 6 times. (18 dc)

Round 4: (Dc in next 2 sts, 2dc in next st) 6 times. (24 dc)

Round 5: (Dc in next 3 sts, 2dc in next st) 6 times. (30 dc)

Round 6: (Dc in next 4 sts, 2dc in next st) 6 times. (36 dc)

Round 7: Dc around.

Round 8: (Dc2tog, dc in next 4 sts) 6 times. (30 dc)

Round 9: (Dc2tog, dc in next 3 sts) 6 times. (24 dc)

Round 10: Change to pink, dc around, slip st to first dc.

Round 11: *Ch4, dtr into same st, (2dtr in next st) twice, dtr, ch4, slip st to same st as last dtr, slip st to next st. Rep from * 6 times.

Fasten off.

Flower chart

Stellar

This pincushion needs nothing more than a pretty stitch. Once the purl cluster has been mastered, it's an easy stitch to remember. The reverse stocking stitch edging is as effective on the wrong side as it is on the right side.

Strap

The strap can be adjusted. The strap needs to cover the base of the flower. If it doesn't, just add more chains to the foundation row to make it wider.

Using purple work as follows:

Foundation row: Ch9, ch3, tr in fourth tr from hook, tr in each ch, ch3, turn.

Row 1: Tr in each st, ch3, turn.

Rep Row 1 until strap is long enough to go around wrist with an overlap for the toggle fastening.

Assembly and finishing

Sew the polka dot button in the middle of the flower. Decorate around the button with lazy daisy stitches in pink. Stuff the centre of the flower. Sew the flower to the middle of the strap, making sure that the strap covers the back of the flower.

Sew the toggle button to the strap.

Panels – make two

Cast on 25 sts.

Row 1: Knit.

Row 2: P1, (pc, p1) to end.

Row 3: Knit.

Row 4: P3, *pc, p1* to last 2 sts, p2.

Rep these four rows until work measures the desired size.

Cast off on a knit row.

Edging

Cast on 5 sts.

Row 1: Knit.

Row 2: Slip 1, p4.

Row 3: K1, kfb 3 times, k1. (8 sts)

Row 4: Cast off 3 sts purlwise, p to end.

These 4 rows make the pattern.

Work until edging is desired length when slightly stretched, ending on a Row 4.

Cast off.

Assembly and finishing

If the edging has started to curl it can be blocked.

Sew the two sides together, stuffing as you work the fourth side.

Slipstitch the edging in place.

SKILL LEVEL

Tools & Materials

Hand-dyed 4-ply wool:
45.75m (50yds)

Knitting needles:
2.75mm (US size 2)

Hollowfibre filling

Special abbreviation

pc = purl cluster – purl 3 sts together, leave on left-hand needle, yarn over needle, purl the stitches again this time removing them from needle.

From Little Acorns

This tiny acorn pincushion is knitted in the round and easily shaped. Blackberry stitch is worked to give added texture. Don't be put off by the long instructions for the leaves; every row is knit, and the shaping is simply cast on and cast off.

SKILL LEVEL

Tools & Materials

DK wool:

A brown: 10m (11yds)

B cream: 5.5m (6yds)

C yellow: 8.25m (9yds)

Knitting needles:

3mm (US size 2/3) straight needles

3mm (US size 2/3) double-pointed needles

Twine

Hollowfibre filling

Acorn bowl

Using A and straight needles, cast on 28 sts.

Row 1: Purl.

Row 2: *(K1, p1, k1) all in next st, p3tog, rep from * to end.

Row 3: Purl.

Row 4: *P3tog, (k1, p1, k1) all in next st, rep from * to end.

These four rows form patt.

Rep until work measures 3.75cm (1½in).

Knit 2 rows.

Cast off.

Acorn top

Using B and double-pointed needles, cast on 24 sts and divide over three needles.

Row 1: Knit.

Row 2: Purl.

Cont in st st until work measures 3.75cm (1½in).

Next row: K2tog to end.

Next row: K2tog to end.

Thread working yarn through last 6 sts and pull tightly together.

Acorn stalk (i-cord)

Using A and two double-pointed needles, cast on 2 sts.

Row 1: Knit, slide sts to other end of needle, keep thread behind the work ready to knit next row.

Rep this row until the work measures 2.5cm (1in).

Cast off.

Leaf

Using A and two double-pointed needles, cast on 3 sts and make an i-cord as for stalk until work measures 5cm (2in).

Join in C and change to single-pointed needles.

The centre stitch is worked in A. Slip this st on odd rows and purl it on even rows, putting yarn C to the back before purling and then bringing it to the front to knit the rest of the row.

Row 1: K1C, sl1A, k1C.

Row 2: K1C, p1A, k1C.

Row 3: Cast on 2C, cast off 2C, sl1A, k1C.

Row 4: Cast on 2C, cast off 2C, p1A, k1C.

Row 5: K1C, sl1A, k1C.

Row 6: Cast on 4C, k5C (these include cast-on sts), p1A, k1C.

Row 7: Cast on 4C, k5C, sl1A, k in C to end.

Row 8: K5C, p1A, k5C.

Row 9: Cast on 2C, k7C, sl1A, k in C to end.

Row 10: Cast on 2C, k7C, p1A, k in C to end.

Row 11: K2togC, k5C, sl1A, k in C to end.

Row 12: K6C, p1A, kC to end.

Row 13: Cast off 3, k2C, sl1A, k in C to end.

Row 14: Cast off 3, K2C, p1A, k in C to end.

Row 15: K3C, sl1A, k3C.

Row 16: K3C, p1A, k3C.

Row 17: Cast on 2C, k5C, sl1A, k in C to end.

Row 18: Cast on 2C, k5C, p1A, kC to end.

Row 19: K5C, sl1A, k5C.

Row 20: K5C, p1A, k5C.

Row 21: K2togC, k3C, sl1A, k in C to last 2 sts, k2togC.

Row 22: K4C, p1A, k4C.

Row 23: Cast off 2, kC to end, break off A.

Row 24: Cast off 2, k to end.

Rows 25–26: Knit.

Rows 27–28: K2tog, k to end.

Cast off.

Assembly and finishing

Sew the side seam of the bowl together.

Sew the acorn top inside the bowl. Stuff the acorn.

Sew running sts on the cast-on edge of the acorn bowl. Gather the base of the bowl together. Sew on the i-cord so that it lies inside the bowl. Ensure the acorn is fully stuffed before fastening the bowl tightly.

Tie the leaves and acorn together with twine.

Sweet Lavender

Nothing relaxes more than the sweet smell of lavender. Add a few lavender seeds to the pincushion filling and the scent will be delicately released while you work.

Cushion – make two

Using green and 2.75mm (US size 2) knitting needles, cast on 23 sts.

Work in st st until your piece is square.

Cast off on a knit row.

Eyelet trim

Using cream and 2mm (US size 0) knitting needles, cast on 4 sts.

Row 1: K1, yo, k2tog, yo, k1. (5 sts)

Row 2: Knit.

Row 3: K2, yo, k2tog, yo, k1. (6 sts)

Row 4: Knit.

Row 5: K1, yo, k2tog, yo, k2tog, yo, k1. (7 sts)

Row 6: Cast off 3 sts, k to end. (4 sts)

These 6 rows form the pattern.

Continue until trim is desired length to wrap around the pincushion.

Assembly and finishing

Add lavender seeds evenly to the filling. Sew sides of pincushion together, stuffing as you complete the fourth side.

Pin the trim diagonally across the pincushion to join at the back. Slipstitch in place.

Add a sprig of lavender to the trim, securing with a pretty button.

SKILL LEVEL

Tools & Materials

Hand-dyed 4-ply wool:
A green: 34.75m (38yds)

4-ply merino wool:
B cream: 4.5m (5yds)

Knitting needles: 2mm (US size 0) and 2.75mm (US size 2)

Hollowfibre filling

Lavender seeds

Dried lavender flower

1 button for decoration

Scaredy Cat

Lions aren't half as dangerous as you think they are. Here's one you can stick pins in without being savaged. He's incredibly soft and cuddly too.

SKILL LEVEL

Tools & Materials

Aran wool and alpaca blend:
Camel: 101m (110yds)

DK wool:
Brown: 3.75m (145in)

Fine metallic thread: 3m (120in)

Crochet hook: 4mm (US size 6) and 3.5mm (US size 4/E)

Steel hook: 1.75mm (US size 4)

Stitch marker to mark the first stitch of the row

Cotton wadding

Hollowfibre filling

Back and sides

These are worked as one with Aran yarn and a 4mm (US size 6) crochet hook.

Round 1: Ch2, 6dc in second st from hook (place marker in first dc to mark start of row; remember to move it at the start of each round).

Round 2: Ch1, dc in same st, (2dc in each st) 5 times, slip st to first ch. (12 dc)

Round 3: Ch1, 2dc next st, (dc in next st, 2dc in next st) 5 times, slip st to first ch. (18 dc)

Round 4: Ch1, dc in next st, 2dc in next st, (dc in next 2 sts, 2dc in next st) 5 times, slip st to first ch. (24 dc)

Round 5: Ch1, dc in next 2 sts, 2dc in next st, (dc in next 3 sts, 2dc in next st) 5 times, slip st to first ch. (30 dc)

Round 6: Ch1, dc in next 3 sts, 2dc in next st, (dc in next 4 sts, 2dc in next st) 5 times, slip st to first ch. (36 dc)

Round 7: Ch1, dc in next 4 sts, 2dc in next st, (dc in next 5 sts, 2dc in next st) 5 times, slip st to first ch. (42 dc)

Round 8: Ch1, dc in next 5 sts, 2dc in next st, (dc in next 6 sts, 2dc in next st) 5 times, slip st to first ch. (48 dc)

Round 9: Ch1, dc in next 6 sts, 2dc in next st, (dc in next 7 sts, 2dc in next st) 5 times, slip st to first ch. (54 dc)

Round 10: Ch1, dc in each st in the row, slip st to first ch. (54 dc)

Round 11: Ch1, back post dc in all sts.

Round 12: Ch1, dc in all sts, slip st to first ch (this forms the first round of the side).

Repeat round 12 until work measures 2cm (¾in). Fasten off and weave in ends.

Face

Work first 10 rows of back. Do not fasten off but leave working stitch loose to pick up for the join.

Nose

Use brown and a 3.5mm (US size 4/E) hook.

Begin with a sliding loop.

Round 1: Slip st, ch2, 4tr, 1htr, 1tr, 1htr, 4tr in the loop, ch2, slip st in the loop, pull loop shut.

Fasten off leaving a long tail for sewing. Weave in centre end.

Eyes – make 2

Using brown and a 3.5mm (US size 4/E) hook.

Begin with a sliding loop.

Round 1: Slip st, ch2, 11hdc in ring, slip st to top of ch2, pull loop shut.

Fasten off leaving a long tail of sewing. Weave in centre end.

Whiskers – make 6

Using fine metallic thread and a 1.75mm (US size 4) steel hook, cut two pieces 4cm (10in) long and work with double thread.

Ch15 or length of whisker required.

Fasten off leaving a tail for sewing in.

Assembly and finishing

Cut circles of wadding to the diameter of the back base and to the depth of the sides.

Sew nose and eyes into position on the face with a slip stitch.

Attach whiskers to the nose. The ends of yarn at the beginning of the chain can be snipped to within 1cm (½in) of the first chain. Weave in all ends.

With the face uppermost insert a 4mm (US size 6) hook into the working loop. Starting with a ch1, attach the face to the last round

of the side with a double crochet join. Insert the cotton wadding when reaching the halfway mark. Insert additional hollowfibre filling to make a more rounded face. Slipstitch to first ch and continue for border.

Border

Ch1, (skip 1, 3tr, 1dtr, 3tr in the same st, skip 1, 1dc in next st) to end omitting the last dc and slip st to first ch.

Fasten off and weave the end into the reverse of the border.

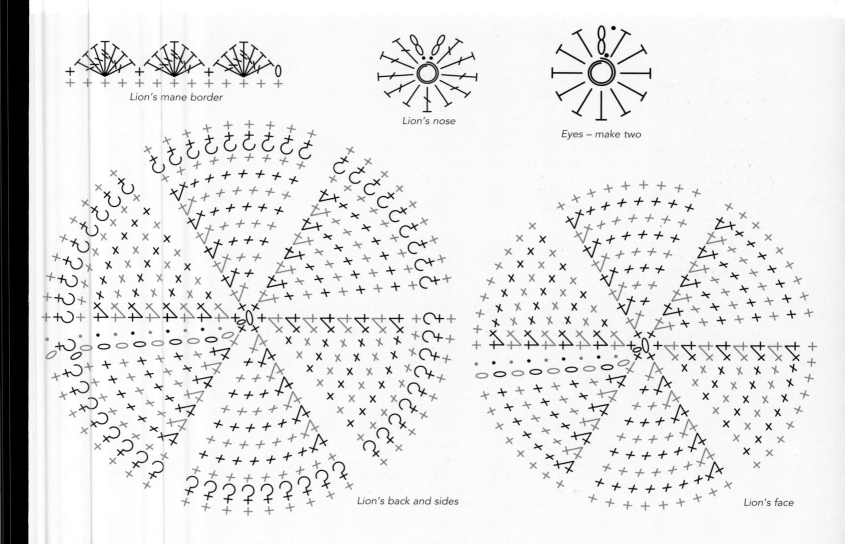

Lion's mane border

Lion's nose

Eyes – make two

Lion's back and sides

Lion's face

Cornflower

Bachelor's button, boutonnière flower, basket flower – there are so many names for this popular flower head. Bring a little of the meadow indoors with this pretty, spike-stitch pincushion.

SKILL LEVEL

Tools & Materials

Aran cotton:
Turquoise: 23.75m (26yds)
Yellow: 1.2m (48in)
Deep blue: 3.65m (4yds)
Crochet hook: 4mm (US size 6)
Hollowfibre filling
Cotton fabric for insert
Sewing thread and needle

Front

Begin with a sliding loop.

Round 1: In yellow slip st, ch2, (counts as first htr) 11hdc in the loop, slip st to top of ch2, pull loop to close but not completely shut to leave room for spike sts. (12 htr)

Round 2: Change colour to turquoise, ch3 (counts as first tr), tr in same st, tr in next st, 1spike tr into the ring, (2tr in next st, tr in next st, 1spike tr into ring) 5 times, slip st to top of ch3. (24 tr)

Round 3: Change colour to deep blue, ch3, 2tr in next st, (tr in next st, 2tr in next st) 11 times, slip st to top of ch3. (36 tr)

Round 4: Change colour to turquoise, ch3, tr in next st, tr and 1spike tr in next st (take spike tr to bottom of V-shaped stitch made by increase in previous round), (tr in next 2 sts, tr and 1spike tr in next st) 11 times, slip st to top of ch3. (48 tr includes 12 spike tr)

Weave in ends but do not fasten off. Leave the working stitch loose for the join.

Back

Basic 12-stitch circle.

Using turquoise, begin with a sliding loop.

Round 1: Slip st, ch3 (counts a first tr) 11dc in the loop, slip st to top of ch3, pull loop shut. (12 tr)

Round 2: Ch3, tr in same st, (2tr in next st) 11 times, slip st to top of ch3. (24 tr)

Round 3: Ch3, 2tr in next st, (tr in next st, 2tr in next st) 11 times, slip st to top of ch3. (36 tr)

Round 4: Ch3, tr in next st, 2tr in next st, (tr in next 2 sts, 2tr in next st) 11 times, slip st to top of ch3. (48 tr)

With front facing, insert the hook into the working loop. Attach the back to the front with wrong sides together. Ch1 to begin a double crochet join. Insert the filled cotton casing when halfway round (see page 17 for 'fabric inserts'). Fasten off and weave ends into the reverse.

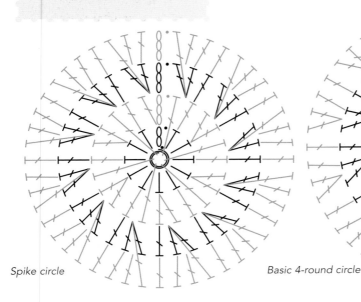

Spike circle

Basic 4-round circle

Dianthus Pinks

Tiny pink flowers nestle tightly together in this pincushion – you can almost smell the sweet perfume. Made from a basic simple square, this pattern is a great way to master the technique before moving on to a bigger project.

Basic square – make 12

Begin with a sliding loop.

Round 1: Slip st, ch3 (counts as first tr), 2tr in ring, (ch2, 3tr in ring) 3 times, join with htr to top of ch3, pull loop shut. (3 tr each side)

Round 2: Ch3, tr in space formed by htr, tr in top of ch3, tr in next 2 sts, 2tr in ch2 space, (ch2, 2tr in the space, tr in next 3 sts, 2tr in next ch2 space) 3 times, ch2, join with slip st to top of ch3 to complete the round. (7 tr in each side)

Fasten off. Weave in the ends and block.

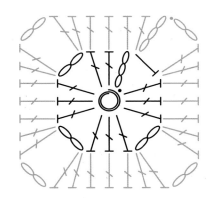

Assembly and finishing

Set out the squares in a grid, two squares by three squares, differing the arrangement on either side. Join the individual squares together with a slipstitch join. Pin the two sides with wrong sides together. With the front facing, join with double crochet putting three stitches in each corner. Insert the filled cotton casing before joining the final side (see page 17 for 'fabric inserts').

SKILL LEVEL

Tools & Materials

DK mercerised cotton:
6 toning shades
3.2m (126in) for each square
21.75m (24yds) in colour chosen for joining
Crochet hook: 2mm (US size 1)
Hollowfibre filling
Cotton fabric for insert
Sewing thread and needle

Round and Around

This perfect sphere is embroidered with lazy daisy stitches. Decorate the pincushion with twisting vines and buds with a pop of yellow French knots to add texture.

SKILL LEVEL

Tools & Materials

DK organic cotton:

Tangerine: 4.75m (16yds)

DK mercerised cotton:

Purple: 1.25m (50in)

Green: 1.25m (50in)

Yellow: 1.25m (50in)

Sewing needle

Hollowfibre filling

Stitch marker

Sphere

This is worked in a spiral without a chain start to the round. Using a stitch marker in the first stitch in the round will make it easier to count the increases.

The sphere should cup in. If your work is loose, you might have to work one row of double crochet and continue increasing in the next round.

Foundation round: Ch2, 6dc in second st from hook. (6 dc)

Round 2: 2dc in each st. (12 dc)

Round 3: (Dc in next st, 2dc in next st) 6 times. (18 dc)

Round 4: (Dc in next 2 sts, 2dc in next st) 6 times. (24 dc)

Round 5: (Dc in next 3 sts, 2dc in next st) 6 times. (30 dc)

Round 6: (Dc in next 4 sts, 2dc in next st) 6 times. (36 dc)

Round 7: (Dc in next 5 sts, 2dc in next st) 6 times. (42 dc)

Round 8: (Dc in next 6 sts, 2dc in next st) 6 times. (48 dc)

Rounds 9–11: Dc in each st (if the end of the first chain isn't on the inside of the sphere, sew it through now).

Decrease rounds

The stitch marker will not mark the first stitch of the round here but can be used as an aid to keeping track of your decreases. Start stuffing the sphere with hollowfibre filling as you decrease, making sure that it is full before fastening off.

Round 12: (Dc2tog, dc in next 6 sts) 6 times.

Round 13: (Dc2tog, dc in next 5 sts) 6 times.

Round 14: (Dc2tog, dc in next 4 sts) 6 times.

Round 15: (Dc2tog, dc in next 3 sts) 6 times.

Round 16: (Dc2tog, dc in next 2 sts) 6 times.

Round 17: (Dc2tog, dc in next st) 6 times.

Round 18: Dc2tog 6 times.

Thread a blunt-ended needle and gather the remaining stitches together to close the sphere. Fasten off and weave end in.

Assembly and finishing

In purple, embroider a large flower on the top of the sphere using lazy daisy stitch.

Stitch four stems with running stitch, placing a single lazy daisy stitch leaf along the length.

Finish the stems with buds of single lazy daisy stitch in purple.

Add French knots in yellow to the buds and large flower centre.

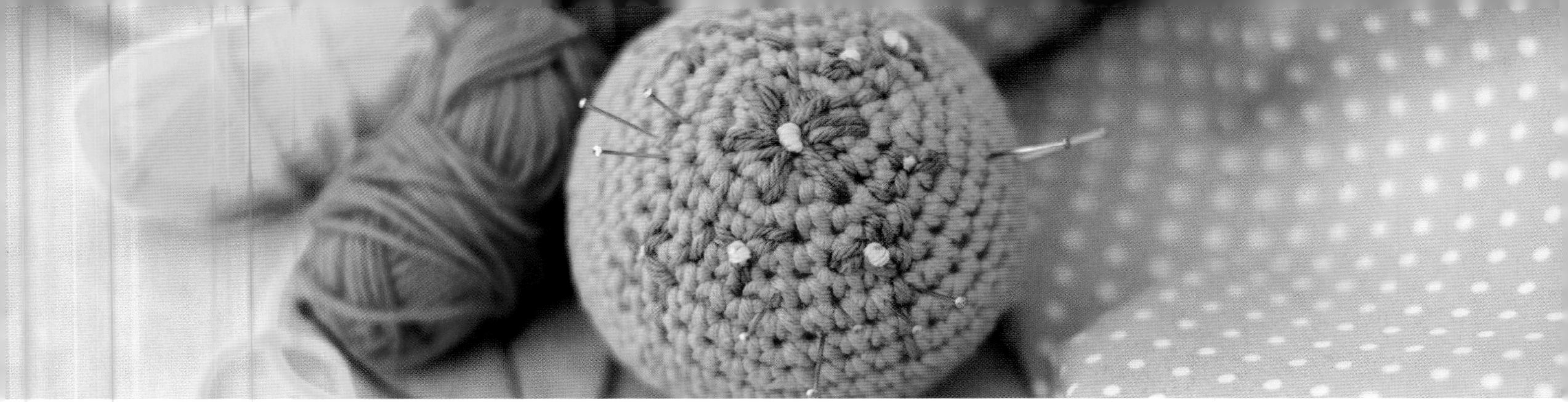

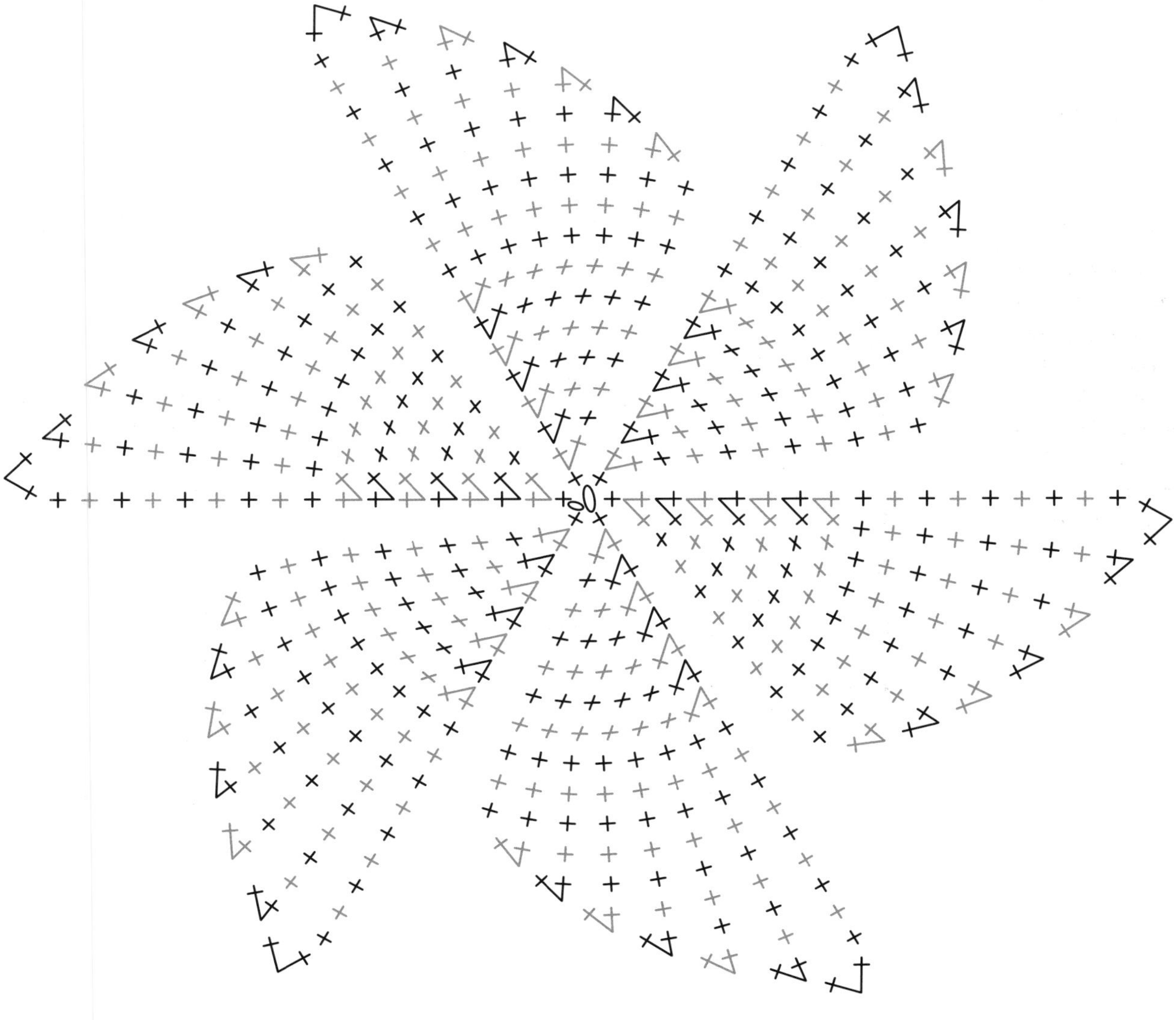

Unstuck

Inspired by the 1960s and the Pop Art movement, this cushion has sliding circles to hide away your pins and needles. Have some funky, retro fun and go dotty with your choice of colours.

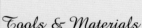

SKILL LEVEL

Tools & Materials

Aran cotton:

Cream: 3.8m (150in)

Orange: 8m (300in)

Yellow: 27.75m (30yds)

Crochet hook: 4mm (US size 6)

1 wooden button

Hollowfibre filling

Front and back

Make two circles using yellow, completing four rounds of the pattern for each circle.

Begin with a sliding loop.

Round 1: Slip st, ch3 (counts as first tr), 11dc in the loop, slip st to ch3, pull loop tight. (12 tr)

Round 2: Ch3, tr in same st, 2tr in each st, slip st to top of ch3. (24 tr)

Round 3: Ch3, 2tr in next st, (tr in next st, 2tr in the next st) 11 times, slip st to top of ch3. (36 tr)

Round 4: Ch3, tr in next st, 2tr in next st, (tr in next 2 sts, 2tr in next st) 11 times, slip st to top of ch3. (48 tr)

Fasten off one circle only. Leave the working stitch on the other circle loose to pick up when joining. Weave in ends.

Work one circle in cream, completing two rounds of the pattern.

Fasten off and weave in ends.

Work one circle in orange, completing three rounds of the pattern.

Fasten off and weave in ends.

Assembly and finishing

Sew cream circle to edge of the orange circle on the right side.

Sew orange circle to edge of last row of the unfastened yellow circle.

Sew wooden button to edge of cream circle.

Reinsert hook in the working loop and, with wrong sides together, attach both yellow circles together with a double crochet join. Stuff with hollowfibre filling as you go.

Fasten off and weave in ends on the reverse.

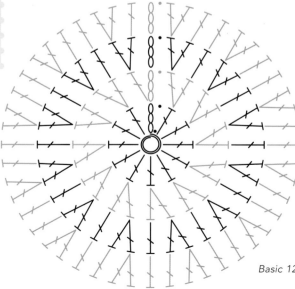

Basic 12-stitch circle

Zigzag Flowers

This pretty pattern is commonly seen in knitting from the Faroe Islands and Iceland. The use of the red, white and green palette gives it a Christmas feel. A dainty picot edging together with a tiny flower and leaves complete the look.

Panel – make two

Using A, cast on 19 sts.

Row 1: (K3A, k1B) 4 times, k3A.

Row 2: P2A, (p3B, p1A) 4 times, p1A.

Row 3: As Row 1.

Row 4: P3A, (p1C, p3A) 4 times.

Row 5: K1A, (k1B, k3A) 4 times, k1B, k1A.

Row 6: (P3B, p1A) 4 times, p3B.

Row 7: As Row 5.

Row 8: P1A, (p1C, p3A) 4 times p1C, p1A.

Rep Rows 1–8 twice more.

Cast off in A.

Edging

Using A, cast on 4 sts.

Row 1: Cast off 2 sts, k1.

Row 2: Knit.

Row 3: Cast on 2 sts.

These 3 rows form the pattern. Continue until the edging is the desired length to fit around the pincushion.

Leaf – make two

Using B cast on 3 sts.

Row 1: Knit.

Row 2: Purl.

Row 3: Kfb, k1, m1b, k1.

Row 4: Purl.

Row 5: Skpo, k1, k2tog.

Row 6: Purl.

Row 7: Slip 1, k2tog, psso.

Assembly and finishing

Weave in all ends and block front and back.

Sew front to back. Start to stuff with hollowfibre filling when working the fourth side. Attach the edging sewing with a slip stitch. Sew on the button and leaves.

SKILL LEVEL

Tools & Materials

DK wool:

A cream: 25m (27yds)

B green: 8.25m (9yds)

C red: 4.5m (5yds)

Knitting needles: 3mm (US size 2/3)

Hollowfibre filling

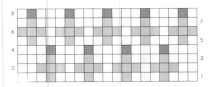

Buttoned Down Granny

This different take on a traditional granny square allows you to make the iconic pattern but with a twist. Just make the number of rounds that cover your pad and allow extra to fold down the corners to meet in the middle, envelope style.

SKILL LEVEL

Tools & Materials

DK cotton:

Green: 17.25m (18¾yds)

Pink: 21.5m (23yds)

Purple: 32.25m (35yds)

Crochet hook: 3.5mm (US size 4/E)

2 toning buttons

Hollowfibre filling

Cotton fabric for insert

Sewing thread and needle

Granny square

In this pattern the stitches are worked in the spaces of the row beneath. To give a neater finish, join in new yarn in a different ch2 space on each round.

Foundation row: Using green begin with ch6, join to first ch with a slip st to form a ring.

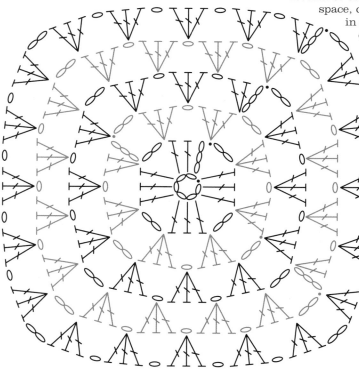

Round 1: Ch3, (counts as first tr), 2tr in the ring, (ch2, 3tr in ring) 3 times, ch2, slip st to top of ch3. (4 tr groups)

Round 2: Change to pink, join in any ch2 space, ch3, 2tr in same space, (ch1, 3tr, ch2, 3tr in next ch2 space) 3 times, ch1, 3tr, in next ch2 space, ch2, slip st to top of ch3. (8 tr groups)

Round 3: Change to purple in any ch2 space, ch3, 2tr in same space, (ch1, 3tr in next ch1 space, ch1, 3tr in next ch1 space, ch2, 3tr in same ch2 space) 3 times, ch1, 3tr in next ch1 space, ch1, 3tr in next ch2 space, ch2, slip st to top of ch3. (3 tr groups each side)

Round 4: Change to green in any ch2 space, ch3, 2tr in same space, (ch1, 3tr in next ch1 space, ch1, 3tr in next ch1 space, ch1, 3tr in next ch2 space, ch2, 3tr in same space) 3 times, (ch1, 3tr in ch1 space) twice, ch1, 3tr in ch2 space, ch2, slip st top of ch3. (4 tr groups each side)

Round 5: Change to pink in any ch2 space, ch3 (counts as first tr), 2tr in same space, *(ch1, 3tr in next ch1 space) 3 times**, ch1, 3tr in next ch2 space, ch2, 3tr in same space***, repeat from * to *** twice, then repeat from * to ** once more, ch1, 3tr in ch2 space, ch2, slip st top of ch3. (5 tr groups each side)

This sets the pattern for increasing the size of the granny square. On every consecutive round there should be one extra set of treble crochets on the side edge of your square. Continue until you have reached the size required.

Final edging round

Continue with the yarn used in the last round of your square, ch1, dc in each st working 3dc in each corner to form a neat turn, slip st to ch1.

Fasten off leaving a long tail for sewing up. Weave in ends.

Assembly and finishing

Place the filled insert on the square and fold the corners of the square into middle (see page 17 for 'fabric inserts'). Thread a blunt needle and attach the edges together using a slipstitch. Sew buttons in the middle of the front and back. Pull tightly together before finishing off.

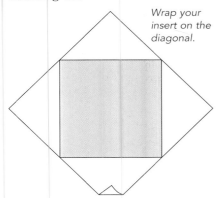

Wrap your insert on the diagonal.

Bubbles

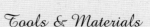

Add splashes of bright colour to a plain background with bubbly bobbles. They are easy to make and add texture to double crochet pieces.

Front

Foundation row: Ch25, ch1, dc in second ch from hook, dc in each ch, ch1, turn.

Row 1: Dc across row, ch1, turn.

Repeat Row 1 until work measures 3.75cm (1½in) ending on a right side row.

Bobble row: With wrong side facing dc in next 2 sts, MB, (dc in next 4 sts, MB) 4 times, dc in next 2 sts, ch1, turn.

Repeat Row 1 until work measures 7.5cm (3in).

Leave the last working stitch loose to pick up again when joining. Tie off the threads of the bobbles to secure. Weave in ends.

Back

Foundation row: Ch25, ch1, dc in second ch from hook, dc in each ch, ch1, turn.

Row 1: Dc across row, ch1, turn.

Repeat row 1 until work measures 7.5cm (3in).

Fasten off and weave in ends.

MB=Make bobble: These 5 stitch bobbles are made by incomplete treble crochets and finished by a treble that draws through all the loops on the hook.

(Yrh, insert hook, pull yarn through, yrh, pull through 2 loops) 5 times, yrh, pull through all 6 loops.

Bobble-row chart

SKILL LEVEL

Tools & Materials

Aran cotton:

Main colour: cream 91.5m (100yds)

Turquoise, pink, green, orange, blue for bobbles: 50cm (20in) of each

Crochet hook: 4mm (US size 6)

Hollowfibre filling

Assembly and finishing

Pin the front to the back with the front facing and wrong sides together.

Reinsert hook in the working loop and attach front to back with a double crochet join. Work 3dc in each corner for neat turns.

Stuff with hollowfibre filling as the third side is completed, paying particular attention to the corners.

Daisy, Daisy

Whether you love them or love them not, daisies in a ring epitomise summer. To make it easier, flower ric rac is sewn around the middle for the perfect daisy chain.

SKILL LEVEL

Tools & Materials

Mercerised cotton:

Blue: 29.25m (32yds)

Crochet hook: 2.75mm (US size C)

Flower ric rac

White, yellow and green embroidery floss

Embroidery needle

Hollowfibre filling

This is worked in a spiral without a chain start to the round. Using a stitch marker in the first stitch in the round will make it easier to count the increases.

The sphere should cup in. If your work is loose, you might have to work one row of double crochet and continue increasing in the next round.

Foundation round: Ch2, 6dc in second st from hook. (6 dc)

Round 2: 2dc in each st. (12 dc)

Round 3: (Dc, 2dc in next st) 6 times. (18 dc)

Round 4: (Dc in next 2 sts, 2dc in next st) 6 times. (24 dc)

Round 5: (Dc in next 3 sts, 2dc in next st) 6 times. (30 dc)

Round 6: (Dc in next 4 sts, 2dc in next st) 6 times. (36 dc)

Round 7: (Dc in next 5 sts, 2dc in next st) 6 times. (42 dc)

Round 8: (Dc in next 6 sts, 2dc in next st) 6 times. (48 dc)

Rounds 9–15: Dc in each st (if the end of the first chain isn't on the inside of the sphere, sew it through now).

Start filling the sphere with stuffing as you decrease making sure that it is full before fastening off.

Round 16: (Dc2tog, dc in next 6 sts) 6 times. (42 dc)

Round 17: (Dc2tog, dc in next 5 sts) 6 times. (36 dc)

Round 18: (Dc2tog, dc in next 4 sts) 6 times. (30 dc)

Round 19: (Dc2tog, dc in next 3 sts) 6 times. (24 dc)

Round 20: (Dc2tog, dc in next 2 sts) 6 times. (18 dc)

Round 21: (Dc2tog, dc) 6 times. (12 dc)

Round 22: (Dc2tog) 6 times. (6 dc)

Thread a blunt-ended needle and gather rem sts together to close the sphere. Fasten off and weave end in.

Assembly and finishing

Embroider both ends using three strands of embroidery floss. With white work lazy daisy stitches for the flowers. With yellow work French knots for centres.

With green, work back stitches for stems.

Sew flowered ric rac around the centre of the sphere.

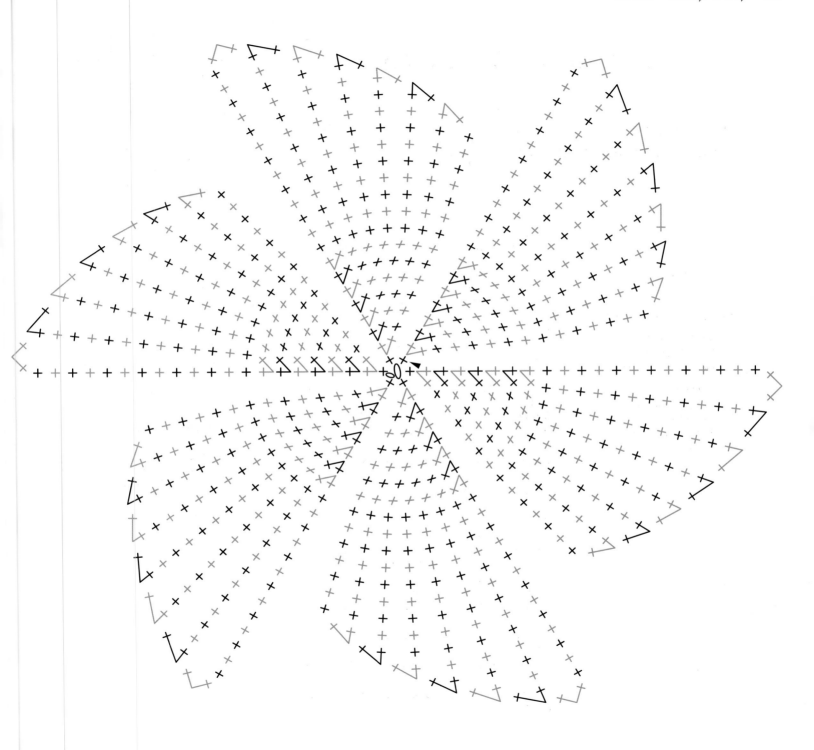

Reindeer

Here is a classic traditional Norwegian design for the perfect reindeer. He stands under heavy, snowfilled skies with a scattering of flakes around him. Time to bring him in from the cold!

SKILL LEVEL

Tools & Materials

DK pure new wool:
A grey: 26m (28yds)
B cream: 5m (5½yds)
Knitting needles: 3mm (US size 3)
Cotton wadding
Hollowfibre filling

Front

Using A, cast on 24 sts.

Row 1: Join in B, k1B, k1A to end.

Row 2: P1B, p1A to end.

Row 3. K1B, k1A to the end. Break off B.

Row 4: Purl in A.

Row 5: Join in B where indicated, k3A, k2B, k1A, k2B, k2A, k2B, k1A, k2B, k9A.

Row 6: P10A, p1B, p2A, p1B, p3A, p1B, p2A, p1B, p3A.

Row 7: K3A, k1B, k2A, k1B, k3A, k1B, k2A, k1B, k10A. *Here*

Row 8: P10A, p1B, p2A, p1B, p3A, p1B, p2A, p1B, p3A.

Row 9: K3A, k2B, k1A, k1B, k3A, k1B, k2A, k1B, k10A.

Row 10: P9A, p12B, p3A.

Row 11: K4A, k12B, k8A.

Row 12: P4A, p2B, p2A, p12B, p4A.

Row 13: K4A, k16B, k4A.

Row 14: P5A, p16B, p3A. (Break off B and rejoin in next row where indicated.)

Row 15: K15A, (join B) k3B, k6A.

Row 16: P7A, p1B, p16A.

Row 17: K13A, k7B, k4A.

Row 18: P5A, p1B, p1A, p1B, p3A, p1B, p12A.

Row 19: K12A, k1B, k3A, k1B, k2A, k1B, k4A.

Row 20: P7A, p1B, p3A, p1B, p12A.

Row 21: K12A, k1B, k2A, k1B, k1A, k1B, k6A.

Row 22: P5A, p1B, p2A, p1B, p1A, p1B, p1A, p1B, p11A.

Row 23: K10A, k1B, k2A, k1B, break off B, k10A to end.

Row 24: Using A only, purl.

Row 25: Knit.

Row 26: Purl.

Row 27: Rejoin B, (k1A, k1B) to end.

Row 28: (P1A, p1B) to end.

Row 29: (K1A, k1B) to end.

Row 30: (P1A, p1B) to end.

Cast off in A.

Back

Using A, cast on 24 sts.

Row 1: Knit.

Row 2: Purl.

These 2 rows form st st.

Cont in st st for 30 rows.

Cast off on next k row.

Assembly and finishing

Weave in ends and block finished pieces but do not press.

Cut wadding to size.

Join the cast-on edge, side seam and cast-off edge. Insert cotton wadding filling with hollowfibre filling for a more rounded shape. Sew up final seam.

Weave in ends into reverse.

Snow in Summer

Summer in the high mountains means snow-capped peaks and wild flowers in the valleys. Use pure new wool and decorate with French knots and tiny bullion stitches.

Both sides are the same. Using A, cast on 26 sts.

Row 1: Knit.

Row 2: Purl.

Row 3: Skpo, k to last 2 sts, k2tog. (24 sts)

Row 4: Purl.

Row 5: Knit.

Row 6: Purl.

Repeat Rows 3–6 three times.

Join B where indicated, leaving a tail for weaving in.

Row 19: Skpo in A, k3A, k1B, k to last 2 sts in A, k2tog in A. (16 sts)

Row 20: P10A, p3B, p3A.

Row 21: K2A, k5B, k5A, k1B, k3A.

Row 22: P2A, p3B, p3A, p to end in B.

Row 23: Skpo in B, k7B, k1A, k to last 2 sts in B, k2tog in B.

Break off A and work with B only.

Row 24. Purl.

Row 25 Skpo, k to last 2 sts, k2tog.

Rep last two rows until 2 sts rem, k2tog.

Assembly and finishing

Fasten off and weave in ends.

Using a mixture of French knots and tiny bullion stitches, decorate the lower slopes of the mountain.

Cut triangular pieces of wadding to size.

With right sides together, attach the front and back. Join the sides of the mountain using mattress stitch, inserting the cotton wadding before completing the third side. Infill with hollowfibre filling to ensure firm corners.

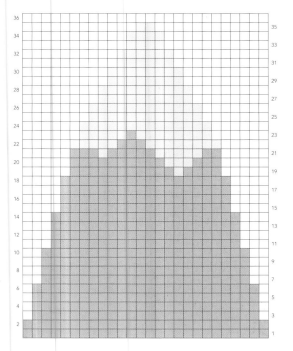

Chain of Flowers

A beautiful posy of flowers is gathered together in a hoop.
Add a few upturned leaves and tiny buttons and it becomes
pretty enough for a wall hanging.

SKILL LEVEL

Tools & Materials

DK organic cotton:
Tangerine: 43m (47yds)
Green: 2.5m (100in)

DK mercerised cotton:
Cream: 7.6m (300in)
Mauve: 2m (73in)
Crochet hook: 3mm (US size C/D)
and 2mm (US size 1/B)
10cm (4in) embroidery hoop
Cotton wadding
Hollowfibre filling
Thin cork
12 tiny tangerine buttons
1 small cream button
Yellow sewing thread and needle

See the basic 12-stitch circle chart
on page 69

Front

Begin with a sliding loop.

Round 1: Slip st, ch3, (counts a first tr),
11dc, slip st to top of ch3, pull loop shut.
(12 tr)

Round 2: Ch3, tr in same st, (2tr in next st)
11 times, slip st to top of ch3. (24 tr)

Round 3: Ch3, 2tr in next st, (tr in next st,
2tr in next st) 11 times, slip st to top of ch3.
(36 tr)

Round 4: Ch3, tr in next st, 2tr in next st,
(tr in next 2 sts, 2tr in next st) 11 times, slip
st to top of ch3. (48 tr)

Round 5: Ch3, tr in next 2 sts, 2tr in next st,
(tr in next 3 sts, 2tr in next st) 11 times, slip
st to top of ch3. (60 tr)

Complete the number of rounds required
until work measures 10cm (4in) in diameter.
Work two rows without increasing. This
will start cupping, making fitting in the
hoop easier.

Fasten off and weave ends in.

Back

Work as for the front until work measures
10cm (4in) in diameter. Fasten off leaving a
long tail for sewing. Weave in ends.

Simple flower – make 12

Using cream mercerised cotton and 2mm
(US size 1/B) crochet hook, begin with
sliding loop, (slip st, ch5) into the loop
5 times, slip st, pull loop shut.

Fasten off, leaving a tail for sewing.

Large flower

Using mauve mercerised cotton and a
2mm (US size 1/B) crochet hook, begin with
a sliding loop.

Round 1: Slip st, 10sc in loop, pull loop shut,
slip st to first dc.

Round 2: (Ch3, 3tr cluster in next st, ch3,
slip st to next st) 5 times.

Fasten off, leaving a tail for sewing.

Simple leaf – make 3

Use green cotton and a 3mm (US size C/D)
hook.

The leaf is worked around the first
7 chain sts.

Ch7, (working through top loops of the
chains) slip st to top loop of second st
from hook, dc, htr, tr, htr, 2dc in first ch,
(working up the other side of the chains)
htr, tr, htr, dc, slip st to first slip st.

Fasten off, leaving a tail for sewing.

Assembly and finishing

Sew a tiny button to the centre of each cream
flower using yellow thread.

Sew a small cream button to the centre of the
mauve flower using yellow thread.

Arrange the flowers and leaves so that the
mauve flower is in the centre of the front.
Using a blunt-ended needle take all loose
ends through to the wrong side.

Sew the flowers in place by anchoring down
occasional chains.

Sew the leaves in place, slightly cupping them at the double crochet end and leaving the slip stitch end loose to point upwards.

Fix the front inside the hoop. Tighten the screw so that it holds in place.

Cut 10cm (4in) diameter layers of cotton wadding to fit inside the ring. Add hollowfibre filling to the centre so that it is slightly raised. This can be held in place at the back with a thin circle of cork.

With the back piece face up, place it over the cork and stitch to the front piece with a slip stitch.

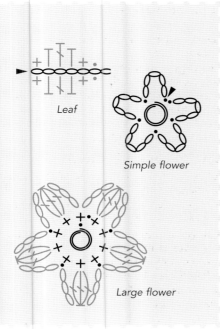

Leaf

Simple flower

Large flower

Deep Water

Make waves with this pincushion, made of super soft merino gathered into pleats. This is a challenging technique that results in a double layer of fabric.

Front

The colours are in two pattern repeat stripes for each of the 5 colours. Change colour at Row 2 of second rep.

Using A cast on 35 sts.

Row 1: K1, (k1, p1) to last 2 sts, k2.

Row 2: K1, p1 to last st, k1.

Row 3: K1, (k1, slip next st on to holder purlwise keeping yarn in front of slip st) to last 2 sts, k2 (keep stitch holder on WS and work with the sts on the needle).

Rows 4, 6 and 8: K1, p to last st, k1.

Rows 5, 7 and 9: Knit.

Row 10: K1, p to last st, k1.

Row 11: Transfer sts on stitch holder on to a 3mm (US size 3) needle so that sts are facing the correct way for working. K1, (k1, p next st from spare needle) rep to last 2 sts, k2.

Repeat Rows 2–11.

Change colour on Row 2 of next patt rep.

When desired length is reached finish the whole of the patt rep.

Cast off in rib on what would be Row 2 of patt.

Back

Cast on 20 sts.

Beg with a k row and cont in st st until back measures same as front.

Cast off leaving a long tail for sewing together.

SKILL LEVEL

Tools & Materials

4-ply merino wool:
A dark blue (also used for the back): 22.75m (25yds)
B mid-blue: 8.25m (9yds)
C aqua: 8.25m (9yds)
D grey: 8.25m (9yds)
E cream: 8.25m (9yds)
Knitting needles:
Three 3mm (US size 3)
Stitch holder
Cotton wadding

Assembly and finishing

Weave in all side ends.

Cut cotton wadding to fit.

With right sides together sew up cast-on edge, one side and cast-off edge. Turn work to right side and insert cotton wadding. Sew up fourth side with right sides facing. Weave in ends on reverse.

Ice Blue

Blue cotton on linen gives the freshness of an icy morning. The lace crochet doily is appliquéd diagonally on to a linen pad and finished off with a chain stitch border for a classic look.

SKILL LEVEL

Tools & Materials

DK mercerised cotton:
9m (10yds)

Crochet hook: 2.5mm (US size B/C)

Two 10cm (4in) squares
of grey linen

Toning thread for sewing

Hollowfibre filling

Crystal motif

Begin with a sliding loop.

Round 1: Ch1, 12sc in loop, slip st to first dc.

Round 2: Ch5 (counts as tr, ch2), (tr, ch2) around, slip st in 3rd of ch5 (12 tr). Pull loop so circle is tighter but not completely shut.

Round 3: Ch3, 1 incomplete tr in next sp, 1 incomplete tr in next tr, pull yarn through (first cluster), ch5, 1 incomplete tr in same st, 1 incomplete tr in next space, 1 incomplete tr in next tr, pull yarn through (cluster), (ch5, cluster) to end, ch2, htr in top of first cluster.

Round 4: Dc in htr space, ch5, dc in next ch-5 sp, ch1, (dc, htr, 3tr, ch3, 3tr, htr, dc, ch1) in next ch-5 sp, *dc in next ch-5 sp, ch5, dc, ch1, (dc, htr, 3tr, ch3, 3tr, htr, dc, ch1) in next ch-5 sp, rep from * 3 times, slip st to first dc.

Fasten off and weave in all ends.

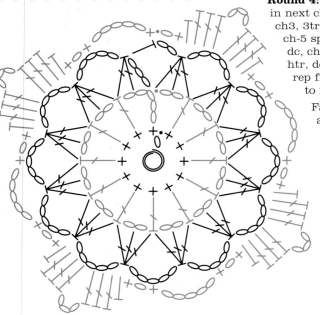

Assembly and finishing

Block the motif. Pin it diagonally and mark out a square on the linen, allowing enough for seams.

Cut out the shape required.

Stitch the motif to RS of linen using a toning sewing thread.

Pin the linen with RS together. Either machine stitch the two pieces or hand sew using backstitch, taking care not to stitch over the motif. Leave enough of a gap on one side to turn the fabric inside out. Stuff with hollowfibre filling and slipstitch the gap.

Chain edging: Ch10, slip st to fifth ch from hook. This forms the corner picot. As you work the chain, use a slip stitch to join it to the edge of the linen.

Work a dc into the corner of the motif as it meets the edge. Place a picot in each corner by slipstitching to fifth chain from hook.

Continue around pad, joining with a slip st to the first ch.

How to crochet a cluster stitch

Incomplete treble crochet: *Yo, insert hook into sp or st specified, yo, pull through (3 loops on hook), yo and pull through 2 loops (this is 1 incomplete tr – there will be 2 loops still on hook). Rep from * as many times as stated, and finish off by working final stage of regular tr to join incomplete tr sts together into a cluster.

Coffee and Cream

Appliquéd cream bunting and flowers on a natural linen background hide an interior that includes a needle holder. The neutral linen cover is kept shut with a popcorn flower button.

Motifs

Bunting

Ch9, (dc in second ch from hook, htr in next ch, tr in next 2ch, ch6) rep until bunting is required length.

Bud

Ch4, 3 incomplete tr in fourth ch from hook, pull yarn through to complete a 4-st cluster.

Five petal flower

Begin with a sliding loop.

Slip st in loop, ch3, 2tr, 2dc in loop, (3tr, 2dc in loop) 4 times, slip st to first ch, pull loop shut.

Popcorn flower

Begin with a sliding loop.

Round 1: Slip st in loop, ch1, 6dc in loop, slip st to first dc.

Round 2: Ch3, 4tr in same st, take hook out of loop, pull yarn through from front of ch3, ch1, (popcorn in next st, ch1) 5 times, slip st to first dc, pull loop shut.

Stems

The stems can be lengthened by adding extra chain sts between the picot leaves. Twist the chain between each slip st so that the leaves are on either side of the stem.

Short stem

Ch9, slip st in 4th ch from hook (picot), ch4, slip st in 4th ch from hook (picot), ch4.

Medium stem

Ch10, slip st in 5th ch from hook (picot), ch6, slip st in 5th ch from hook (picot), ch3.

Long stem

Ch12, slip st in 5th ch from hook (picot), ch7, slip st in 5th stem from hook (picot), ch6.

Assembly and finishing

Cut the cream linen and lining material into an 20 x 10cm (8 x 4in) oblong.

Arrange the bunting diagonally across the linen, making sure the flags are not caught in the seam allowance. Stitch with small running stitches in toning thread.

Fold the linen in half and place the stems on the right-hand side. Stitch to secure. Sew the bud on the shortest stem, the five petal flower on the medium stem and the popcorn flower on the longest stem. The popcorn flower will be used as the button, so place it close to the edge without catching it in the seam.

To make the fastening, chain a length long enough to be looped and sewn into the seam on the opposite side edge to fit around the popcorn flower. Sew in place.

Cut two oblongs of felt for the needle holder. Fold the lining material in half and backstitch the felt oblongs in place on the fold line.

With RS together stitch the linen front to the lining, leaving a gap to turn through the right way. Finish the gap with a slip stitch.

SKILL LEVEL

Tools & Materials

Natural organic cotton crochet thread: 14m (15yds)

Crochet hook: 2.5mm (US size B/C)

Cream linen

Contrast cotton for lining

Two felt squares in contrasting colours

Sewing needle and toning sewing thread

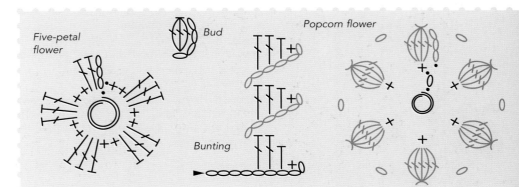

Five-petal flower

Bud

Popcorn flower

Bunting

Beehive

This is a great way to make your essential equipment more attractive. The bee hides a retractable measuring tape that stays fixed to the pincushion. It fits snugly between the hexagon cells when not in use.

Hexagon – make 4

Using yellow and begin with a sliding loop.

Round 1: Ch3, tr, (ch2, tr in loop) 5 times, htr into top of ch3.

Round 2: Ch3, tr in top of ch3 in previous rnd, tr in next st, tr in next space, (ch2, tr in same sp, tr in next 2 sts, tr in next sp) 5 times, ch2, slip st to top of ch3.

Bee – tape cover

There is no need to break off yarn at the end of rnds as it is carried up the back of the work.

Foundation row: Using yellow, ch12, slip st to first ch to form a ring.

Round 1: Ch2, htr in each ch in foundation row, slip st to top of ch2. (12hdc)

Round 2: Without breaking off yellow join in black, ch2, htr in same st, 2htr in each st, slip st to top of ch2. (24 htr)

Round 3: Using yellow ch2, htr in same st, htr in next st, (2htr in next st, htr in next st) to end, slip st to top of ch2. (36 htr)

Round 4: Using black, ch2, htr in each st to end, slip st to top of ch2.

Round 5: Using yellow ch2, htr2tog, (htr in next st, htr2tog) to end, slip st to top of ch2.

Insert the tape before finishing the decrease rows.

Round 6: Using black, ch2, (htr2tog) to end, slip st to top of ch2.

Round 7: Using yellow, ch2, htr around, slip st to top of ch2.

Round 8: Using yellow, ch2, htr2tog to end. Gather sts together and fasten off.

Wings – make 2

Using white and 3.5mm (US size E) hook, ch8, dc in second st from hook, working into each ch in turn, htr, tr, dtr, tr, htr, dc, fasten off leaving a tail for sewing.

Antennae – make 2

Using black and 3.5mm (US size E) hook, ch6, slip st in each ch, fasten off leaving a tail for sewing.

Assembly and finishing

Join two hexagons for the top and another two for the bottom. Insert stuffed felt casing (see page 17 for 'fabric inserts').

Starting with the top, rejoin yarn in last round, ch1, working into back loop only dc around the two hexagons, place two dc in each corner.

Work 4 rnds in dc working into back loop only.

Attach to the bottom with a slip stitch join, stuffing as you go.

Add extra definition to the top by finishing with a slip stitch border.

Join the yarn to the final round and slipstitch around the pincushion.

Sew wings to the bee. Sew on two antennae and work French knots for the eyes and mouth. Joining yellow in a stitch underneath the bee, make a chain the desired length and slipstitch to the underneath of the hexagons.

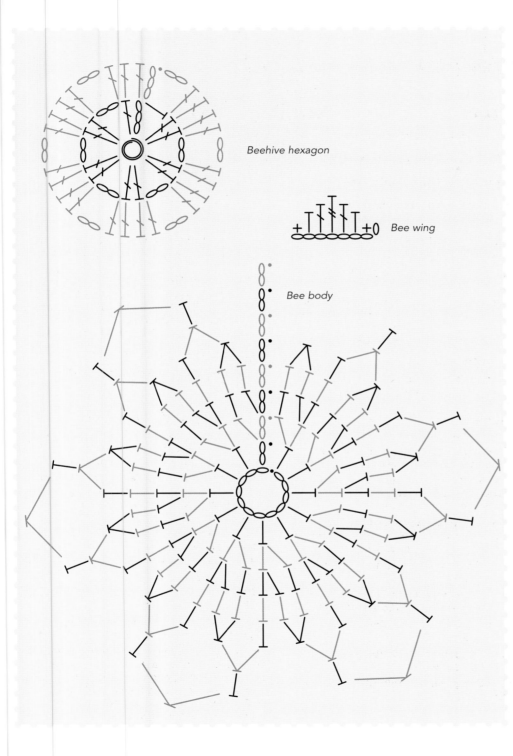

Beehive hexagon

Bee wing

Bee body

Got to Love Cats

Wild cats have beautiful coats that come in a whole host of patterns and colourways. Go feral with neons or cream for a sophisticated snow leopard. The choice is yours.

SKILL LEVEL

Tools & Materials

4-ply wool:
A pink: 27.5m (30yds)
B grey: 24.75m (27yds)
Knitting needles: 3mm
(US size 2/3)
Cotton wadding
Hollowfibre filling
Pipe cleaner for tail
2 green jewel beads for eyes
1 black bead for the nose

Front and back – both alike

Either follow the chart or the written instructions below for print pattern.

Using A, cast on 30 sts.

Row 1: K3B, k4A, k2B, k4A, k4B, k4A, k3B, k4A, k2B.

Row 2: P3B, p2A, p2B, p1A, p2B, p2A, p5B, p2A, p6B, p3A, p2B.

Row 3: K4A, k2B, k3A, k2B, k2A, k1B, k3A, k1B, k1A, k2B, k3A, k2B, k4A.

Row 4: P3A, p2B, p3A, p3B, p1A, p5B, p2A, p2B, p3A, p3B, p3A.

Row 5: K3A, k3B, k4A, k2B, k7A, k4B, k2A, k2B, k3A.

Row 6: P4A, p1B, p2A, p3B, p3A, p2B, p3A, p3B, p3A, p2B, p4A.

Row 7: K3B, k2A, k1B, k3A, k2B, k3A, k4B, k4A, k4B, k4A.

Row 8: P1B, p4A, p2B, p4A, p1B, p3A, p1B, p4A, p5B, p5A.

Row 9: K13A, k2B, k3A, k2B, k7A, k3B.

Row 10: P3B, p6A, p3B, p2A, p3B, p2A, p2B p5A, p3B, p1A.

Row 11: K1A, k1B, k1A, k3B, k2A, k4B, k2A, k3B, k2A, k3B, k5A, k1B, k2A.

Row 12: P2A, p2B, p5A, p5B, p3A, p2B, p2A, p1B, p2A, p3B, p1A, p2B.

Row 13: K2B, k2A, k2B, k1A, k2B, k2A, k1B, k13A, k3B, k2A.

Row 14: P4A, p2B, p4A, p2B, p4A, p3B, p1A, p3B, p2A, p2B, p1A, p2B.

Row 15: K5B, k2A, k3B, k1A, k2B, k3A, k5B, k3A, k2B, k4A.

Row 16: P5B, p3A, p3B, p2A, p2B, p2A, p5B, p4A, p3B, p1A.

Row 17: K9A, k2B, k4A, k2B, k3A, k2B, k3A, k3B, k2A.

Row 18: P8A, p2B, p3A, p3B, p4A, p1B, p3A, p2B, p4A.

Row 19: K3A, k4B, k7A, k2B, k3A, k2B, k9A.

Row 20: P3A, p3B, p3A, p3B, p1A, p3B, p6A, p2B, p2A, p2B, p2A.

Row 21: K3A, k1B, k2A, k3B, k7A, k3B, k4A, k2B, k1A, k1B, k3A.

Row 22: P2A, p2B, p2A, p2B, p4A, p1B, p7A, p2B, p3A, p2B, p3A.

Row 23: K3A, k2B, k3A, k3B, k10A, k2B, k2A, k2B, k3A.

Row 24: P3A, p6B, p5A, p1B, p5A, p2B, p2A, p3B, p3A.

Row 25: K4A, k5B, k5A, k3B, k6A, k2B, k5A.

Row 26: P6A, p1B, p4A, p3B, p2A, p2B, p5A, p2B, p5A.

Row 27: Cast off in A.

Cat's tail – make one

Either follow the chart or the written instructions below.

Using B, cast on 8 sts leaving a tail for sewing up.

Row 1: Knit.

Row 2: Purl.

Row 3: As Row 1.

Row 4: As Row 2.

Row 5: K2B, k2A, k4B.

Row 6: P3B, p3A, p2B.

Row 7: K3B, k2A, k3B.

Row 8: P2B, p3A, p3B.

Row 9: K2B, k4A, k2B.

Row 10: P1B, p5A, p2B.

Row 11: K2B, k5A, k1B.

Row 12: P all sts B.

Row 13: K all sts B.

Row 14: P3B, p2A, p3B.

Row 15: K2B, k3A, k3B.

Row 16: P7B, p1B.

Row 17: K3A, k3B, k2A.

Row 18: P1A, p5B, p2A.

Row 19: K1A, k3B, k4A.

Row 20: P3A, p3B, p2A.

Row 21: K2A, k6B.

Row 22: P all sts B.

Row 23: K4B, k1A, k3B.

Row 24: P3B, p1A, p4B.

Row 25: K3B, k2A, k3B.

Row 26: P2B, p4A, p2B.

Row 27: K1B, k5A, k2B.

Row 28: P all sts A.

Row 29: K all sts A.

Row 30: P all sts A.

Row 31: K all sts B.

Row 32: P all sts B.

Row 33: K5B, k1A, k2B.

Row 34: P2B, p2A, p4B.

Row 35: K3B, k4A, k1B.

Row 36: P1B, p5A, p2B.

Row 37: K all sts A.

Row 38: P all sts A.

Row 39: K2A, k2B, k4A.

Row 40: P1A, p4B, p3A.

Row 41: K all sts B.

Row 42: P all sts B.

Cast off in B, leaving a length for sewing.

Assembly and finishing

Weave in all loose ends.

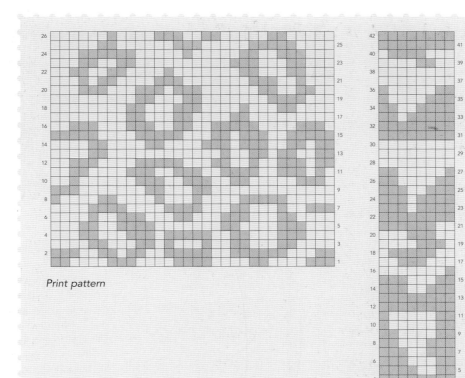

Print pattern

Cat's tail

Tail

Bend the top end of the pipe cleaner slightly to avoid a sharp edge. Wrap cotton wadding around the pipe cleaner and lay on the length of the tail piece.

Using the long end left on the cast-on edge, gather up the edge tightly around the pipe cleaner. Sew up the seam of the tail.

Set aside to sew into the right-hand seam of the body.

Body

Cut cotton wadding to size.

Lay both knitted pieces with right sides together and sew up the cast-off edge, left-hand seam and cast-on seam. Insert cotton wadding, adding hollowfibre filling for shaping.

Sew the tail to the right-hand seam and complete the join.

On both sides of the top seam, measure out the placement for the top-stitched ears. On the top seam, measure 3.75cm (1½in) from the edge and mark. On the side seams 3.25cm (1¼in) from the top. Using B, sew with running stitch to join the two points.

Sew on jewel eyes and bead nose.

Weave in ends.

Mr Bear

No animals were hurt in the making of this pincushion! Hang Mr Bear from a handy hook in your workroom. Or, if you keep your pins close to your chest, sew on a fastener and use him as a cameo. He's very versatile.

SKILL LEVEL

Tools & Materials

DK pure new wool:
Cream: 17.25m (19yds)
Grey: 23m (25yds)
Mustard: 5m (5½yds)
Crochet hook: 3mm (US size C/D) and 2.5mm (US size B/C)
Stitch markers
Black embroidery thread
Sewing needle
Hollowfibre filling
Cotton wadding

Face

This is worked in a spiral so there are no joining stitches. Use stitch markers to keep count of rounds. Using cream and 2.5mm (US size B/C) hook, work as follows:

Foundation round: Ch2, 6dc in second st from hook. (6 dc)

Round 2: 2dc in each st. (12 dc)

Round 3: (Dc in next st, 2dc in next st) 6 times. (18 dc)

Round 4: (Dc in next 2 sts, 2dc in next st) 6 times. (24 dc)

Round 5: (Dc in next 3 sts, 2dc in next st) 6 times. (30 dc)

Round 6: (Dc in next 4 sts, 2dc in next st) 6 times. (36 dc)

Rounds 7–8: Dc around.

If the end of first ch isn't on the inside, sew it through now. Begin stuffing with hollowfibre filling as you decrease.

Round 9: (Dc2tog, dc in next 4 sts) 6 times. (30 dc)

Round 10: (Dc2tog, dc in next 3 sts) 6 times. (24 dc)

Round 11: (Dc2tog, dc in next 2 sts) 6 times. (18 dc)

Round 12: (Dc2tog, dc in next st) 6 times. (12 dc)

Round 13: Dc2tog 6 times. (6 dc)

Fasten off.

Ears – make two

Using cream and 2.5mm (US size B/C) hook, ch2, 6dc in second st from hook, ch1, turn. (6 dc)

Row 1: 2dc in each st, ch1, turn. (12 dc)

Row 2: Dc2tog 6 times.

Fasten off.

Muzzle

Using cream and 2.5mm (US size B/C) hook, ch2, 6dc in second st from hook. (6 dc)

Round 1: 2dc in each st. (12 dc)

Round 2: (Dc in next st, 2dc in next st) 6 times. (18 dc)

Round 3: (Dc in next 2 sts, 2dc in next st) 6 times. (24 dc)

Round 4: (Dc2tog, dc in next 2 sts) 6 times. (12 dc)

Fasten off.

Plaque – make two

Using grey and 3mm (US size C/D) hook, ch8.

Round 1: Ch5, ch3 (first tr), tr in fourth ch from hook, tr in top loop of next 3ch, 7tr in first ch, working on other side of ch, tr in next 3 sts, 5tr in same ch as first tr, slip st to top of ch3.

Round 2: Ch3, tr in next 6 sts, 3tr in next 3 sts, tr in next 7 sts, 3tr in next 3 sts, slip st to top of ch3.

Round 3: Ch3, tr in next 6 sts, 2tr in next st, tr, (2tr in next 2 sts, tr) twice, 2tr in next st, tr in next 7 sts, 2tr in next st, tr, (2tr in next 2 sts, tr) twice, 2tr in next st, slip st to top of ch3.

Round 4: Ch3, tr in next 8 sts, (2tr in next st, tr) 6 times, tr in next 10 sts, (2tr in next st, tr) 6 times, tr, slip st to top of ch3.

Fasten off on one side only. Weave in ends.

Assembly and finishing

Pin two plaque pieces together with wrong sides together and a piece of cotton wadding sandwiched between them. Attach the pieces together with a double crochet join.

With mustard, work a row of surface chains around the edge of the plaque before working on the edging.

Plaque edging

Working into the surface chain, dc, (ch3, skip 1, dc on next surface ch) around, join to first dc with a slip st.

Attach ears to the side of the face.

Embroider features on muzzle before attaching to face. Stuff muzzle slightly with hollowfibre filling before completing the join. Embroider eyes.

Sew the face to the plaque with a slip stitch using the same yarn as the face.

Weave in all ends.

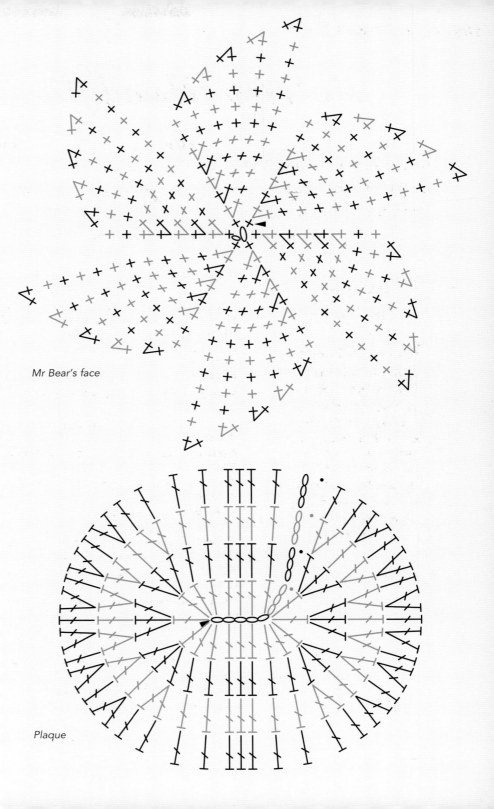

Mr Bear's face

Plaque

Flower Mandala

'Mandala' is Sanskrit for circle and is used to symbolise the universe. The radial balance of this motif begins at the centre and spirals down to the end. In this pincushion, the colours have been chosen to represent a stained glass rose window.

SKILL LEVEL

Tools & Materials

4-ply cotton:
Green: 36cm (14in)
Purple: 10m (11yds)
Mauve: 3m (2½yds)
Pink: 3.75m (4yds)
Turquoise blue: 2m (2¼yds)
Crochet hook: 2.75mm (US size C)
Cotton fabric for lining
Sewing needle and toning
   sewing thread
Hollowfibre filling

Motif

With so many changes in colour, it might be easier to weave the ends in as you go.

Row 1: Using green, ch5, slip st to first ch to form loop.

Row 2: Ch1, 8dc in loop, slip st to first dc.

Row 3: Using purple, join yarn in back loop of any dc in previous row, ch3 (counts as first tr), tr in back loop of same st, ch1,

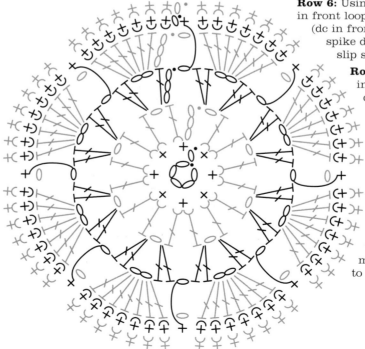

(2tr in back loop of next st, ch1) to end, slip st to top of ch3. (16 tr)

Row 4: Using mauve, join yarn in any ch-1 sp, ch3, tr, ch2, 2tr in same space, *(ch1, 2tr, ch2, 2tr) in next ch space, rep from * to end, ch1, slip st to top of ch3.

Row 5: Using pink, join yarn in any ch-2 sp, ch3, 6tr in same ch-2 space, ch1, (forms first cluster), (7tr in next ch-2 sp, ch1) to end, slip st to top of ch3.

Row 6: Using turquoise blue, join yarn in front loop of first tr in a cluster, ch1, (dc in front loop of each tr in cluster, spike dc in ch-1 sp in Rnd 4) to end, slip st to first dc.

Row 7: Using purple, join yarn in back loop of first tr in a cluster, ch1, dc in back loop of each tr in Rnd 5, slip st to first dc.

Weave in all ends before attaching the cotton lining.

Using the top of the motif as a template, draw around the outside allowing extra for the seams. Use the template to cut a piece of cotton. Fold the seams towards the inside of the motif and slipstitch in place to the inside of the motif.

Azulejo

Geometric blue and white tiles are part of the heritage of Portugal. Create your own pincushion variety with overlaid crochet on a plain cream background.

Decrease rows

You can alter the depth of the pincushion by gradually decreasing, working a round of double crochet between each decrease round if needed. Remember to mark the first stitch in each round.

Start stuffing with hollowfibre filling as you decrease.

Row 8: Mark first st, dc around.

Row 9: (Dc in next 6 sts, dc2tog) to end.

Row 10: (Dc in next 5 sts, dc2tog) to end.

Row 11: (Dc in next 4 sts, dc2tog) to end.

Row 12: (Dc in next 3 sts, dc2tog) to end.

Row 13: Dc around.

Row 14: (Dc in next 2 sts, dc2tog) to end.

Row 15: (Dc, dc2tog) to end.

Row 16: Dc2tog to end.

Assembly and finishing

Stuff the pincushion fully. Using a blunt-ended needle, work a running stitch in each double crochet. Pull the thread to gather the gap and fasten off tightly. Weave the end in.

Front and back

Using cream, ch19, dc in second st from hook.

Row 1: Dc in each ch, ch1, turn.

Row 2: Dc in each st, ch1, turn.

Rep Row 2 until work is square.

Side of tile

Using cream, ch6, dc in second st from hook.

Row 1: Dc in each ch, ch1, turn.

Row 2: Dc in each st, ch1, turn.

Rep Row 2 until work fits around perimeter of square. Do not fasten off yet as it might need to be adjusted.

Assembly and finishing

Using an air-erasable fabric pen, outline the design on to the square. Work a surface chain in blue over the outline.

Using blue, attach the side piece to the front with a double crochet join, putting a spike dc at centre of each side. Work 3dc in each corner.

As you near the end of the side adjust the length.

Join the edges of the sides with a slip stitch.

Using cream, attach the back with a double crochet join.

Insert cotton wadding before joining the final side.

Fasten off and weave in all ends.

SKILL LEVEL

Tools & Materials

DK mercerised cotton:
Cream: 48.5m (53yds)
Blue: 5.5m (6yds)
Crochet hook: 2.75mm (US size C)
Either cotton wadding for filling or a 2.5cm (1in) foam piece
Air-erasable fabric pen

Sushi Style

Which piece will you pick? Laid out on a seaweed base, it's hard to choose from these easy knit and purl patterns!

Seaweed base is knitted in caterpillar stitch.

Top

Using lime green and 3.5mm (US size 4) needles, cast on 33 sts.

Row 1: (P3, k1) to last st, p1.

Row 2: K1, (p1, k3) to end.

Row 3: As Row 1.

Row 4: As Row 2.

Row 5: As Row 1.

Row 6: (K3, p1) to last st, k1.

Row 7: P1, (k1, p3) to end.

Row 8: As Row 6.

Row 9: As Row 7.

Row 10: As Row 6.

These ten rows form the pattern.

Rep Rows 1–9 once more.

Cast off on Row 10 as st presents itself, i.e. cast off p sts purlwise and k sts knitwise.

Bottom

Using lime green and 3.5mm (US size 4) needles, cast on 33 sts.

Row 1: Knit.

Row 2: Purl.

These 2 rows form st st. Cont in st st until work measures same as top.

Cast off on a k row.

Roe ball

This is knitted in Andalusian st as follows:

Using orange and 3.5mm (US size 4) needles, cast on 19 sts.

Row 1: Knit.

Row 2: Purl.

Row 3: Knit.

Row 4: (P1, k1) to last st, p1.

These 4 rows form pattern.

Rep Rows 1–4 twice more.

Row 13: (K2tog) to last st, k1.

Row 14: Purl.

Row 15: As Row 13.

Thread yarn through rem sts and remove from needle.

Egg roll

Using yellow and 2.75mm (US size 2) needles, cast on 11 sts.

Row 1: P1, (slip 1 purlwise, p1) to end.

Row 2: Purl.

Row 3: P2, (slip 1 purlwise, p1) to last st, p1.

Row 4: Purl.

These four rows form the pattern.

Repeat Rows 1–4 until work can be rolled with an overlap to pull centre out. Cast off.

Tuna and rice roll

Using cream and 3.5mm (US size 4) needles, cast on 38 sts.

Row 1: (K1, p1) to end.

Rep until work measures 4cm (1½in).

Cast off in rib.

Using peach, cast on 52 sts and work as for cream.

Crab stick

Using cream and 3.5mm (US size 4) needles, cast on 8 sts.

Work in garter st (every row knit) for 7.5cm (3in).

Join in pink halfway through a row. Changing colour midway through rows, work pink and cream on alternate rows until the section covers the cream centre when rolled.

Fasten off pink and continue in cream only until this section covers last section.

Change to pink for one wrap. Each section should measure the same as the initial roll.

Cast off.

Handy hint

The egg roll can be used to hold scissors or crochet hooks.

Assembly and finishing

Base

Cut the cardboard, to stiffen the base, to size. Wrap with cotton wadding. This can be slipstitched in place.

Sew top of base to bottom, inserting the cardboard when the third side is completed. Sew the fourth side. Weave all ends to reverse.

Roe ball

Thread yarn through cast-on edge and pull tight to close. Sew up the side seam, stuffing with hollowfibre filling as you go. Pull the stitches placed on the yarn together. Finish stuffing before closing the top.

Fasten off and weave ends in.

Egg roll

Use a thick pencil and roll up from the side of the work and pull up the inside of the roll to shape. Place stitches through work to hold in place.

Weave in ends.

Tuna and rice roll

Lay both the cream and peach ribs together with the side of the peach rib slightly overlapping the cream. Roll up so that the peach overlaps the cream at the end of the swirl.

Stitch in place to hold the shape.

Place the finished sushi on the base and stitch in place.

Got It Covered

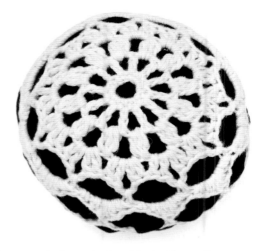

More commonly seen as a covering for pebbles, this lacy motif will make the perfect wrapping for a plain, oval pincushion. Although instructions are given, adjustments for fit can still be made.

SKILL LEVEL

Tools & Materials

Natural organic cotton crochet thread: 24m (26yds)

Crochet hook: 2.5mm (US size B/C)

Cotton fabric for the insert

Hollowfibre filling

Assembly

Fit is everything with this pincushion, so the fabric yoyo insert will need to be completed before the crochet lace motif.

Draw a circle on to the fabric. Use a dinner plate to draw around. Cut out the circle and press a 0.5cm (¼in) seam around the edge. Sew down with running stitch and gather together. Stuff with hollowfibre filling before sewing the edge securely.

Measure your motif against the pad, inserting the pad as you decrease.

Motif

Begin with a sliding loop.

Round 1: Slip st, ch1, 12sc in loop, slip st to first dc.

Round 2: Ch5 (counts as first tr and ch-2 sp), (tr, ch2) to end, slip st to top of ch3.

Round 3: Slip st to next sp, ch3, 2 incomplete tr (see page 100), pull yarn through (beginning cluster), ch3, (3tr cluster in next sp, ch3) to end, slip st to top of first cluster.

Round 4: Slip st to next sp, ch3, tr, ch3, 2tr in same sp, *(2tr, ch3, 2tr) in next sp, rep from * to end, slip st to top of ch3, slip st to next st, slip st to next sp.

Round 5: Dc, ch5, (dc in next sp, ch5) to end, slip st to first dc.

Round 6: Slip st to next space, (dc, htr, 3tr, htr, dc) in same sp, (dc, htr, 3tr, htr, dc) in next sp to end, slip st to first dc.

Round 7: Slip st in next 3 sts, ch7, (dc to second tr in next cluster, ch7) to end, slip st in first slip st.

Round 8: Slip st to next sp, ch5, (dc in next ch-7 sp, ch5) to end, slip st to first slip st.

The cover should start curling in at this point. Depending on the size and amount of filling, you might need to adjust the decreasing to fit the shape.

Round 9: Slip st to next sp, (ch4, dc in next ch-5 sp) to end, slip st to first slip st.

Round 10: Slip st to next sp, (ch3, dc in next ch-4 sp) to end, slip st to first slip st.

Insert pad.

Round 11: Slip st to next sp, 2dc in each sp.

Round 12: Dc around.

Round 13: Dc, (skip 1, dc) around.

When the motif fits, fasten off and leave a long tail. Thread on to a blunt-ended needle, sew a running stitch through the final row of the motif and gather the edge together.

Taste of Honey

When you want to add that special touch to your tea party, hand-decorated sugar cubes are absolutely perfect. This 3D sugar cube decorated with strawberry ric rac and a vintage flower will satisfy the sweetest tooth.

Square – make six
Using yellow cast on 12 sts.
Work in st st until your work is a square.
Cast off on a knit row.

Leaf – make two
Using green cast on 3 sts, leaving a long tail for sewing.
Row 1: Knit.
Row 2: Purl.
Row 3: Kfb, k1, m1b, k1. (5 sts)
Row 4: Purl.
Row 5: Kfb, k3, m1b, k1. (7 sts)
Row 6: Purl.
Row 7: Skpo, k3, k2tog. (5 sts)
Row 8: Purl.
Row 9: Skpo, k1, k2tog. (3 sts)
Row 10: Purl.
Row 11: Sk2po and fasten off.

Assembly and finishing
Cut foam to size.
Join the squares together as set out in the net shape for a cube. Fold into shape at the seams and join the remaining seams. Insert the foam before finishing the last seam.

Sew the ric rac along the bottom. Sew the flower and leaves on to the top of the cube.

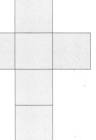

Net shape for the cube

SKILL LEVEL

Tools & Materials
DK mercerised cotton:
Yellow: 20m (22yds)
Green: 1.75m (2yds)
Knitting needles: 2.75mm (US size 2)
Flower button
Ric rac
2.5cm (1in) foam for filling

Special abbreviation
Kfb = knit into front and back of next stitch to increase by 1 stitch

Water Lily

Multi-petalled and multi-layered, the flowers of a water lily can measure up to 30cm (12in) across. In shades of white, pink, yellow, peach and red, their flowers change colour as they age. Pick your favourite colours and float a water lily on its own pond.

SKILL LEVEL

Tools & Materials

Mercerised cotton:

Yellow: 1.8m (2yds)

White: 4.25m (4½yds)

Coral pink: 7.25m (8yds)

Blue: 14.75m (16yds)

1 pearl shank button

Crochet hook: 3mm (US size C/D)

Hollowfibre filling

Layered flower motif

Using yellow, make a sliding loop.

Round 1: Ch1, 8dc in loop.

Round 2: *Ch3, (dtr, tr) in same st, slip st to next dc, repeat from * 8 times, fasten off.

Round 3: Turn work (WS facing). Join in white on any dc post in Rnd 1, slip st around dc post, (ch4, slip st around next dc post) 8 times.

Round 4: Turn work (RS facing), slip st yarn through last loop worked, (ch4, 3dtr in same ch-loop, slip st to next loop) 8 times, fasten off.

Round 5: Turn work (WS facing). Join in coral pink on any dc post in Rnd 1, slip st around dc post, (ch5, slip st around next dc post) 8 times.

Round 6: Turn work (RS facing), slip st yarn through last loop worked, (ch3, tr, dtr, trtr, dtr, 2tr in same ch-loop, slip st to next loop) 8 times.

Round 7: Turn work (WS facing). Join in blue on any dc post in Rnd 1, slip st around dc post, (ch3, slip st around next dc post) 8 times.

Round 8: Turn work (RS facing), slip st yarn through last loop worked, (ch2, 3tr, htr) in same loop, (htr, 3tr, htr all in next loop), 7 times, slip st to top of ch2.

Round 9: Working into each st in turn, ch2, 3tr, htr, (htr, 3tr, htr) to end, slip st to top of ch2.

Round 10: Ch3, working into the back loop only, work 1tr in each st, slip st to top of ch3.

Round 11: Ch3, tr in each st, slip st to top of ch3.

Round 12: Ch3, tr in each st, slip st to top of ch3.

Weave in all ends before starting decrease rows.

Round 13: Ch3, tr2tog, (tr, tr2tog) to end, slip st to top of ch3.

Round 14: Ch3, tr in same st, (tr2tog) to end, slip st to first tr.

Insert hollowfibre filling before closing the final round.

Round 15: Ch3, tr, (tr2tog) to end, slip st to first tr.

Gather up sts with thread and fasten off.

Assembly and finishing

Sew a button in the centre of the flower and tighten it through to the back.

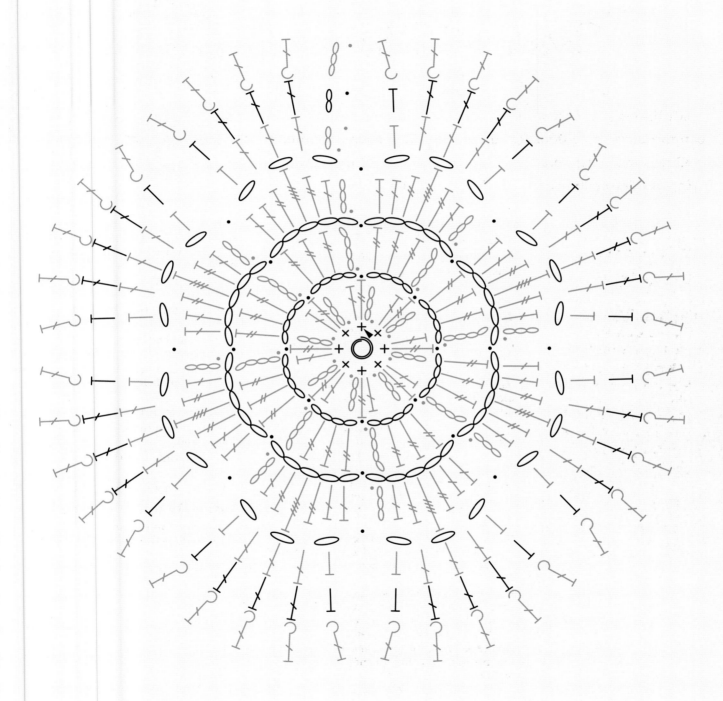

Flora

Inspired by the bright colours of Mexico, this pincushion brings the spirit of fiesta. It is much easier than it looks because the flowers around the middle are simply made of ric rac.

SKILL LEVEL

Tools & Materials

4-ply cotton:

Yellow: 1.4m (1½yds)

Red: 3.25m (3½yds)

Orange: 6m (6½yds)

Green: 11m (12yds)

Crochet hook: 2.75mm (US size C)

Floral ric rac

Toning felt

Sewing thread and needle

Hollowfibre filling

Flower motif – make two

Using yellow, begin with a sliding loop.

Round 1: Ch4 (counts as first tr and ch1 space), (tr, ch1) 11 times, slip st to 3rd ch, fasten off.

Weave in ends.

Round 2: Using red and working into ch1-sp, ch3, 2tr cluster, (ch2, 3tr cluster) 11 times, ch2, slip st to top of ch3, fasten off.

Weave in ends.

Round 3: Using orange and working into ch2-sp, ch3, 2dtr, tr in first space, (tr, 2dtr, tr in next space) 11 times, ss to top of ch3, fasten off.

Weave in ends.

Round 4: Using green ch1, dc in back post of each st, slip st to first ch.

Round 5: Ch3, tr in each st, fasten off.

On one side only.

Round 6: Ch3, tr in each st, do not fasten off.

Assembly and finishing

Weave in all ends.

Cut two circles of felt to act as a fabric backing for the flower motifs. These can be sewn using a slip stitch to hold in place if they move while filling.

Using the working loop on Rnd 6, join the two ends together with a slip stitch, stuffing as you go. Weave ends in. Sew the ric rac around the centre.

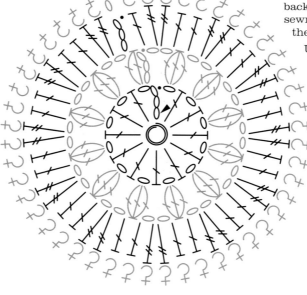

Fly Away Home

These delightful creatures are so widespread and popular that they have many names: ladybug, ladybird, lady beetle, lady clock, lady cow, and lady fly are just a few of the popular ones. In nearly every culture they are thought to bring good luck.

Body – make two

Using black, begin with a sliding loop.

Round 1: Slip st, ch3 (counts as first tr) 11dc into loop, slip st to top of ch3, pull loop tight. (12 tr)

Round 2: Ch3, tr in same st, 2tr in each st, slip st to top of ch3. (24 tr)

Round 3: Ch3, 2tr in next st, (tr, 2tr in next st) 11 times, slip st to top of ch3. (36 tr)

Round 4: Ch3, tr, 2tr in next st, (tr in next 2 sts, 2tr in next st) 11 times, slip st to top of ch3. (48 tr)

Wings – make two

Using red, begin with a sliding loop.

Round 1: Slip st, ch3 (counts as first tr), 11dc into loop, slip st to top of ch3, pull loop tight. (12 tr)

Round 2: Ch3, tr in same st, 2tr in each st, slip st to top of ch3. (24 tr)

Round 3: Ch3, 2tr in next st, (tr, 2tr in next st) 11 times, slip st to top of ch3. (36 tr)

Antennae – make two

Using black, ch6, slip st in each ch, fasten off leaving a tail for sewing.

Assembly and finishing

Body

With wrong sides together, attach the top and bottom with a double crochet join, stuffing as you go. Weave in ends.

Wings

Fold the wings in half and sew to the top of the body. Sew two buttons on to each wing.

Eyes

Place the smaller black button on top of the white button and sew to the front of the body using white thread.

Antennae

Sew each antenna on either side of the eyes.

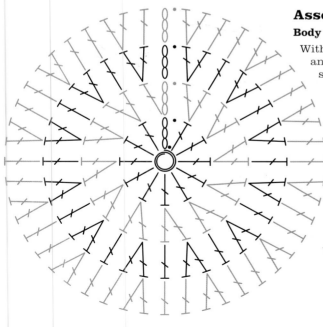

SKILL LEVEL

Tools & Materials

Mercerised cotton:

Black: 16.5m (18yds)

Red: 10m (11yds)

Crochet hook: 2.75mm (US size C)

Four small black buttons for wings

2 white buttons

2 small black buttons for eyes
(to fit inside white buttons)

Hollowfibre filling

Ribbon Lace

Filet crochet has long been associated with delicate thread edging for shelves and ribbons. There are two designs to make and a stepped edging to add.

SKILL LEVEL

Tools & Materials

Natural cotton crochet thread:
34m (37yds)
Steel hook: 1.75mm (US size 4)
Cotton fabric for insert
Hollowfibre filling

Flower block motif

Follow block chart by working 4tr in the full blocks and (tr, ch2, skip 2, tr) in the empty blocks.

Row 1: Ch21, ch3, tr in fourth ch from hook, tr in each ch, ch3, turn. (22 tr)

Row 2: Tr in next 3 sts, (ch2, skip 2, tr) 5 times, tr to end, ch3, turn.

Row 3: Tr in next 3 sts, (ch2, skip 2, tr, 2tr in ch-2 sp, tr) twice, ch2, skip 2, tr to end, ch3, turn.

Row 4: Tr in next 3 sts, (ch2, skip 2, tr) twice, 2tr in ch-2 sp, tr, ch2, skip 2, tr, ch2, skip 2, tr to end, ch3, turn.

Row 5: Tr in next 3 sts, (ch2, skip 2, tr, 2tr in ch-2 sp, tr) twice, ch2, skip 2, tr to end, ch3, turn.

Row 6: Tr in next 3 sts, (ch2, skip 2, tr) 5 times, tr to end, ch3, turn.

Row 7: Tr to end, ch3, turn.

Row 8: Tr in next 3 sts, (ch2, skip 2, tr) 5 times, tr to end, ch3, turn.

Row 9: Tr in next 3 sts, ch2, skip 2, tr, (2tr in ch-2 sp, 1tr) 3 times, ch2, skip 2, tr to end, ch3, turn.

Row 10: Tr in next 3 sts, ch2, (skip 2, tr in next 4 sts) twice, ch2, skip 2, tr to end, ch3, turn.

Row 11: Tr in next 3 sts, ch2, skip 2, tr in next 4 sts, 2tr in ch-2 sp, tr in next 4 sts, ch2, skip 2, tr to end, ch3, turn.

Row 12: Tr in next 3 sts, (ch2, skip 2, tr) 5 times, tr to end, ch3, turn.

Row 13: Tr to end.

Row 14: Slip st in next 3 sts, ch3, tr in next 3 sts, (ch2, skip 2, tr) 3 times, tr in next 3 sts, turn.

Row 15: Slip st in next 3 sts, ch3, 2tr in ch-2 sp, tr, ch2, skip 2, tr, 2tr in ch-2 sp, tr, turn.

Row 16: Slip st in next 3 sts, ch3, 2tr in ch-2 sp, tr.

Double block motif

Row 1: Ch21, ch3, tr in fourth ch from hook, tr in each ch, ch3, turn. (22 tr)

Row 2: Tr in next 3 sts, (ch2, skip 2, tr) 5 times, tr to end, ch3, turn.

Row 3: Tr in next 3 sts, (ch2, skip 2, tr) twice, 2tr in ch-2 sp, tr, (ch2, skip 2, tr) twice, tr to end, ch3, turn.

Row 4: Tr in next 3 sts, ch2, skip 2, tr, 2tr in ch-2 sp, tr in next 4 sts, 2tr in ch-2 sp, tr, ch2, skip 2, tr to end, ch3, turn.

Row 5: Tr in next 3 sts, (ch2, skip 2, tr in next 4 sts) twice, ch2, skip 2, tr to end, ch3, turn.

Row 6: Tr in next 3 sts, ch2, skip 2, tr in next 4 sts, 2tr in ch-2 sp, tr in next 4 sts, ch2, skip 2, tr to end, ch3, turn.

Rows 7–10: Rep Rows 3–6.

Row 11: As Row 3.

Row 12: As Row 2.

Row 13: Tr to end.

Row 14: Slip st in next 3 sts, ch3, tr in next 3 sts, (ch2, skip 2, tr) 3 times, tr in next 3 sts, turn.

Row 15: Slip st in next 3 sts, ch3, 2tr in ch-2 sp, tr, ch2, skip 2, tr, 2tr in ch-2 sp, tr, turn.

Row 16: Slip st in next 3 sts, ch3, 2tr in ch-2 sp, tr.

Bottom edging on both sides

Row 1: Rejoin yarn in fourth st in from foundation row on right-hand side, ch3, tr in next 3 sts, (ch2, skip 2, tr) 3 times, tr in next 3 sts, turn.

Row 2: Slip st in next 3 sts, ch3, 2tr in ch-2 sp, tr, ch2, skip 2, tr in next 4 sts, turn.

Row 3: Slip st in next 3 sts, ch3, 2tr in ch-2 sp, tr.

Assembly and finishing

Use the motif as a template and cut out two pieces of cotton fabric. Stitch together, leaving a gap to turn to the right side. Stuff and slipstitch gap closed.

With wrong sides together, sew together with whip stitch. Insert casing before the fourth edge is joined. Weave ends into the casing.

Bottom edging

Double block motif

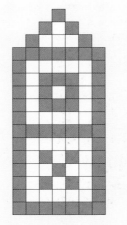

Flower block motif

Chequered Heart

This pretty heart eases you in to shaping in Fair Isle. For something extra special, add rose petals to the filling. Fasten a ribbon to hang in your workroom as a decoration, or slip in with your yarn for gorgeous, scented projects.

SKILL LEVEL

Tools & Materials

DK wool:

A cream: 9m (10yds)

B fuchsia: 4½m (5yds)

C light pink: 4½m (5yds)

Knitting needles: 3.75mm (US size 5)

Hollowfibre filling

Optional:

Rose petals for stuffing

Ribbon for hanging

1 button

Make two

The colours can be carried up the side, reducing the need to weave in ends.

All increases are worked on RS rows.

On purl rows, work each stitch in the colour it presents.

On the increase rows, knit the first stitch and then make 1 st by lifting and working into the strand between the first and second stitches, keeping the colour pattern equal.

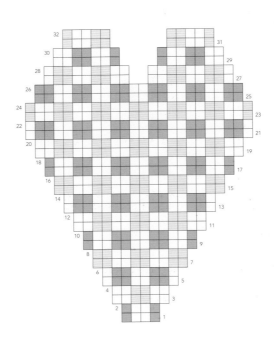

At the end of the row, make 1 st by lifting and working into the strand between the last two stitches, keeping the colour pattern equal.

Knit the last stitch as the colour pattern would suggest.

Using A, cast on 4 sts.

Row 1 (RS): K1B, k2A, k1B.

Row 2 and every following WS row: Purl in colour as stitch presents.

Row 3: K1A, m1fA, K2C, m1bA, k1A.

Row 5: K1A, m1fB, k1B, k2A, k1B, m1bB, k1A.

Row 7: K1C, m1fC, k2A, k2C, k2A, m1bC, k1C.

Row 8: As Row 2.

This sets colour patt.

Cont in patt, increasing on knit rows and purling WS rows for 20 rows.

Row 21: Knit (do not increase).

Row 22: Purl.

Rep last two rows.

Row 25: Skpo, k to last 2 sts, k2tog.

Row 26: Purl.

Row 27: Skpo, k7, k2tog, turn.

Diagonal Square

Math doesn't have to be boring. This very easy pincushion uses simple increases to give a completely different shape to plain knitting. The pretty picot edging gives an introduction to picking up stitches on a selvedge.

Place left side sts on a stitch holder and work on right side only as follows:

*Row 28: P9.

Row 29: Skpo, k3, k2tog.

Row 30: Purl.

Row 31: Skpo, k1, k2tog.

Row 32: Purl.

Cast off.

Slip sts from the stitch holder on to needle and rejoin yarn at the spot where the centre divided to complete the left side.

Left side:

K to last 2 sts, k2tog.

Work as for right side, from * to end.

Assembly and finishing

If using ribbon, fold the ribbon over to make a hanging loop and pin it to the centre top seam.

Starting at the side, sew both sides together, filling as you go.

Sew button to bottom of ribbon.

Make two

Cast on 4 sts.

Row 1: Knit.

Row 2: K2, yo, k to end.

Rep Row 2 until work measures 3.75cm (1½in).

Decrease row: K1, k2tog, yo, k2tog, k to end.

Rep last row until 4 sts remain.

Next row: Knit.

Cast off.

Assembly and finishing

Sew front and back together inside the edge made by the yarn over. Stuff before finishing off.

Sew the buttons on the front and back, pulling them tightly together.

Picot edging

Starting with new yarn, pick up 1 st from the selvedge, working through front and back edges.

*Cast on 2 sts.

Cast off 2 sts.

Pick up next st on edge, pass original stitch over.

Rep from * around pincushion.

SKILL LEVEL

Tools & Materials
Cotton linen blended yarn:
34m (37yds)
Knitting needles: 3mm (US size 2/3)
Hollowfibre filling
2 wooden buttons

Tangerine Dream

The mixture of colours and the ruffle border on this pincushion are reminiscent of vintage pillows. It definitely invites you to rest your head for a sound sleep!

Front

The front of this pincushion is worked in single rows. Each row starts on the right.

Foundation row: In tangerine ch20, dc in second ch from hook, dc in every ch. (19 dc)

Row 1: Green – change colour in first dc of previous row, ch3, (skip 2, tr, 1spike tr into the chain row beneath, tr in same st as first tr) 6 times. (6 tr clusters)

Row 2: Tangerine – change colour in first ch3 space of the previous row, ch3, 1spike tr in first skipped dc in the space in Row 1, tr in same ch3 space, (tr in next space, 1spike tr in first skipped dc in the space in Row 1, tr in same space) 5 times, ch3, slip st to final st in previous row.

Row 3: Green – change colour in first ch3 space of previous row, ch3, (in the next space tr, 1spike tr in the spike tr of previous green row, tr) 6 times.

Row 4: Tangerine – change colour in first ch3 space of the previous row, ch3, 1spike tr in the spike tr in the previous green row, tr in same space, (in the next space tr, 1spike tr in the spike tr of previous row, tr) 5 times, ch3, slip st to final st in previous row.

Rows 3 and 4 form the pattern. Repeat until work is the desired size, ending on Row 4. Do not fasten off as this stitch starts the edging.

Edging

Make an edging of double crochet down the left side. Fasten off when the initial chain row is reached.

Rejoin the yarn at the other end of the chain row and repeat the dc edging up the right side, ensuring the same spread of stitches as the left side. Fasten off when the last treble crochet row is reached. Use a stitch marker to mark this as the point to join the green yarn at the start of the ruffle edging.

Back

In green:

Foundation row: Ch22, ch3, tr in fourth ch from hook, tr in each ch, ch3, turn. (23 tr)

Row 1: Tr in each st, ch3, turn.

Repeat Row 1 until work measures the same as the front. Fasten off and weave in ends.

Assembly and finishing

Pin the front to the back with wrong sides facing.

The border starts with the front facing at the marked point at the top right corner.

Join the green yarn.

Ruffle border

3htr in each st around the edge. On the top edge only, place a spike htr in the spike tr of the previous green row to close the gap.

If the ruffle isn't gathering enough, place 4htr in a st occasionally for a fuller fold. Insert the casing as the third side is completed (see page 17 for 'fabric inserts'). Work around the edge of the pincushion to the first htr, join with a slip stitch. Fasten off and weave the ends in on the reverse.

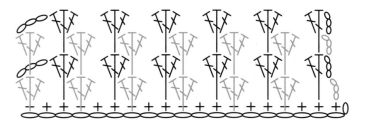

Mint Stripe

This simple five-row stripe pattern has a tight, woven look thanks to the stitch combination. The scalloped border picks out the contrasting pink colour.

Front and back

A single row of colour is worked. The colours can be used in any sequence, but keep to the same colours that you've set out in the first five rows.

Make two, keeping the sequence of rows the same on both sides.

Foundation row: In pale pink ch22.

Row 1: Dc in second st from hook, dc in all sts to end.

Row 2: Change colour, ch2, htr in every st to end.

Row 3: Change colour, ch1, dc in every st to end.

Row 4: As Row 2.

Row 5: As Row 3.

These five rows set the colour change sequence.

Work for the size of pincushion required.

Fasten off.

Weave in ends and block both sides.

Assembly and finishing

Pin the front to the back with wrong sides together. Starting in the second stitch at the beginning of the last row, join hot pink, ch1, work tr across the row, place 3 sts in each corner, join the side seams together. Try to place a stitch in each row. Keep front and back stripes matching.

Once you have joined three sides, start stuffing with hollowfibre filling, paying particular attention to the corners. Slipstitch to first chain, then ch1 ready for the border.

Border: (Dc, skip 2, 5tr in next st, skip 2) to final st, slip st to first dc.

Space the scallops so that you have an equal number on each side and one in each corner. If you need to adjust the spacing, skip one stitch instead of two.

Fasten off and weave in ends on reverse side.

SKILL LEVEL

Tools & Materials

DK organic cotton:

Pale pink: 14.5m (16yds)

Hot pink: 9.5m (10¼yds)

Purple: 9.5m (10¼yds)

Cream: 9.5m (10¼yds)

Mint green: 9.5m (10¼yds)

For border: 9.2m (10yds)

Crochet hook: 3mm (US size C/D)

Hollowfibre filling

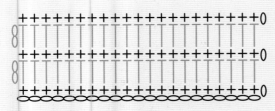

Mint stripe five-row pattern

Scalloped border

Under the Stars: Gemini

This design is simply inspired by our night sky. You can hand embroider your own star sign or that of a friend and give it as a gift.

SKILL LEVEL

Tools & Materials

DK mercerised cotton:

Dark blue: 26m (28½yds)

Crochet hook: 2.75mm (US size C)

Yellow embroidery floss and needle for stitching

Hollowfibre filling

Front and back

Make two octagons.

Begin with sliding loop.

Round 1: Slip st, ch1, 7dc in the loop, slip st to ch1, pull loop tight. (8 dc)

Round 2: Ch1, dc in same st as ch1, 2dc in each st, slip st to ch1. (16 dc)

Round 3: Ch1, 2dc in next st, (dc in next st, 2dc in next st) 7 times, slip st to ch1. (24 dc)

Round 4: Ch1, dc in next st, 2dc in next st, (dc in next 2 sts, 2dc in next st) 7 times, slip st to ch1. (32 dc)

Round 5 Ch1, dc in next 2 sts, 2dc in next st, (dc in next 3 sts, 2dc in next st) 7 times, slip st to ch1. (40 dc)

Round 6: Ch1, dc in next 3 sts, 2dc in next st, (dc in next 4 sts, 2dc in next st) 7 times, slip st to ch1. (48 dc)

Round 7: Ch1, dc in next 4 sts, 2dc in next st, (dc in next 5 sts, 2dc in next st) 7 times, slip st to ch1. (56 dc)

Round 8: Ch1, dc in next 5 sts, 2dc in next st, (dc in next 6 sts, 2dc in next st) 7 times, slip st to ch1. (64 dc)

Fasten off one side only. Leave the working stitch loose for the join.

Weave in ends.

Assembly and finishing

For the hand embroidery, split a length of embroidery floss into three strands. Using the chart as reference, sew the stars with a cross-stitch. Because of the nature of crocheted work, these stitches might not form a perfect cross. When all stars have been sewn, join them with backstitch to form the constellation.

Insert hook in the working loop and, with wrong sides together and front facing, attach top to bottom with a slipstitch join. Add stuffing as you go, ensuring the pincushion is fully stuffed before fastening off.

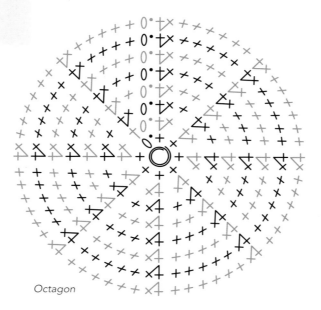

Octagon

Constellation maps

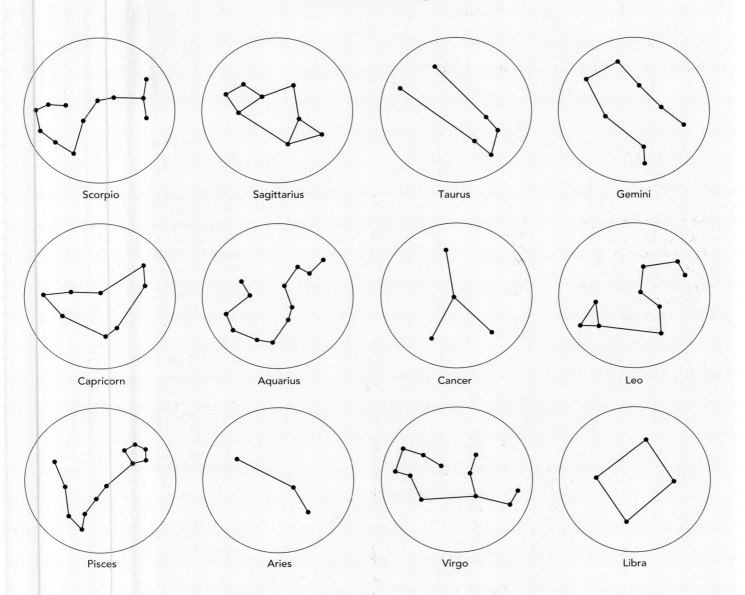

Scorpio

Sagittarius

Taurus

Gemini

Capricorn

Aquarius

Cancer

Leo

Pisces

Aries

Virgo

Libra

Index

Suppliers

Colourway
Market Street
Whitland
Carmarthenshire
Wales
SA34 0AJ
www.colourway.co.uk

Cucumberpatch
59 High Street
Wolstanton
Newcastle under Lyme
Staffordshire
ST5 OER
www.cucumberpatch.co.uk

Fun 2 Do
21 Scotch Street
Carlisle
Cumbria
CA3 8PY
www.fun2do.co.uk

I Knit London
106 Lower Marsh
Waterloo
London
SE1 7AB
www.iknit.org.uk

Kathy's Knits
64a Broughton Street
Edinburgh
EH1 3SA
www.kathysknits.co.uk

The Knitting Hut
65 High Street
Woburn Sands
Buckinghamshire
MK17 8QY
www.theknittinghut.co.uk

Loop
15 Camden Passage
Islington
London
N1 8EA
www.loopknitting.com

The Sheep Shop
72 Beche Road
Cambridge
CB5 8HU
www.sheepshopcambridge.co.uk

Twist Fibre Craft Studio
88 High Street
Newburgh
Cupar
Fife
Scotland
KY14 6AQ
www.twistfibrecraft.co.uk

Yarn on the Square
22 Market Place
Ely
Cambridgeshire
CB7 4NT
www.yarn-on-the-square.co.uk

Credits

Quarto would like to thank both Lion Brand Yarn and Thomas B. Ramsden for providing the yarns used in the making of this book.

Lion Brand Yarn
135 Kero Road
Carlstadt
NJ 07072
USA
www.lionbrand.com

Thomas B. Ramsden & Co. (Bradford) Limited
Netherfield Road
Guiseley
Leeds
LS20 9PD
UK
www.tbramsden.co.uk

All photographs and illustrations are the copyright of Quarto Publishing plc.